DON'T MISS
THE LAST
TRAIN HOME

To Rosalind

Best wishes

Karol
x

DON'T MISS THE LAST TRAIN HOME

Copyright © 2022 Karol Darnell

Publisher Honesty Press - www.honestypress.co.uk

Formatting: Honesty Press
Editors: Honesty Press & Monday Writers.
Front cover graphics by: Chris Connelly.
Author photo: Brian Darnell (c1967)

ISBN: 978-1-7396495-1-7 (Paperback)
978-1-7396495-2-4 (Hardcover)
 978-1-7396495-0-0 (ebook)
First edition: August 2022 - 10 9 8 7 6 5 4 3 2 1

DON'T MISS THE LAST TRAIN HOME

Karol Darnell

Honesty Press
ESTABLISHED 2022
WWW.HONESTYPRESS.CO.UK

For all those who went before,
those who are here,
and those who are yet to come.

All the postcards referred to are taken

from Beatrice's album and can

all be viewed on the publisher's website:

www.honestypress.co.uk

Victorian Failsworth plays its part,
to mould and shape a young girl's heart,
The rocking chair sees grief and tears,
Babies fed and passing years.

Steam trains fast and barges slow,
Mill wheels turn, the workers go
with hungry mouths at home to feed,
Strong young men who toil and bleed.

She sees her brother learn to swim,
And helps him get the rabbits in,
Her songbird sister sweet sixteen,
Her pretty face no longer seen.

She knows the love, she feels the pain,
She sees the sun and senses rain,
Honesty, her favourite flower,
Sweet kisses pass away the hour.

Canal below and train above,
From Wrigley Head she sends her love
to Flanders fields and out of sight,
Her soldier man goes off to fight.

Stylish hats on heads she graces,
Then holidays in seaside places,
Postcards carefully tucked away,
Her memories help her through the day.

Prologue

The hospital room is bright with artificial light and with no access to a window; I have no way of telling what time it is.

The doctor entered the little cubicle looking at his notes in preference to me, his patient.

"Good morning, Mrs Rowland, how are we today?"

"My wrist aches, but I'll manage," I answer politely.

"It was a nasty break for a lady of your... years," he stumbles over those words as if he might offend me.

I smile at him.

"I hope to be able to play my piano again soon."

"Yes, yes," he said holding up the x-ray to the light. "Very important. Now, can you remember your age?"

"I'm ninety," I answer. "I was born on 25th June 1896."

"Your address, Mrs Rowland?"

"Blaen Ty, 164 Broadway, New Moston."

"Very good. You live alone?"

"I do now since my husband died sixteen years ago. We were married for forty-six years." I add, as if I need to justify myself.

"Do you know your alphabet?" He asked, indifferent to the information.

I take a deep breath, and smile to myself.

"A B C D E F G H I J K L M N O P Q R S T U V W X Y Z…Z Y X W V U T S R Q P O N M L K J I H G F E D C B A"

I raise my eyebrows at his bemused face.

"May I go home now?"

"You certainly can Mrs Rowland. I don't think the fall did you any harm at all. Please take care."

He left the cubicle, pulling the curtain back around behind him.

I gather my things and leave the hospital. There is a taxi waiting for me to take me to my home; the home Thomas bought for me all those years ago. My mind is spinning with my thoughts as I open my back door.

Don't miss the last train home

What everyone sees is a ninety-year-old silver haired lady with a broken wrist. Everyone thinks I might have dementia or that I am too old to live alone. What they don't see is me.

Beatrice.

A broken wrist is nothing. A heart, broken many times, now that's a thing harder to mend.

I open the tall cupboard in my kitchen and reach inside for my now old and battered album. It's heavy and that's made more difficult by the cast on my left arm and wrist.

The old rocking chair creaked as I sat down to open my collection of postcards; all the memories of the people I have known, reminders of the loves I have had, and the places I have been. It all comes flooding back with memories so sharp I can taste them.

I know each card as I lift off the well-worn front cover that became detached years ago. I recognise each picture and who sent them; the ones that cheered me and the ones that mended the hurt too, the joyful and the sad.

Slowly, I turn the pages of my album, beautiful silk embroidered cards, photographs, humorous postcards, and so many birthday cards. I search through the randomness of my album. I am searching for the one card. The very first one I ever found and kept precious to me for fear I should lose the memories.

"There you are," I said out loud to the small, printed card.

So much has happened since he left us.

Chapter one

The death of

James

I was only three and a half when my father died.

My giant of a daddy. His dark, slicked-back hair that he tried to contain under his flat cap, moth eared and worn, the original colour a mystery. Dirt, time bonded to his threadbare jacket and his huge hobnailed boots.

"I hear him!" I squealed, jumping up to the sound of him wearily returning from work at the iron foundry along with the shift of mill workers from The Ivy and Wrigley Head Mills. I could hear them clattering down the cobbled streets, their clogs clashing and sparking on the setts.

"Daddy!"

His soft blue eyes, set in his gentle round face, grimy and weary with the day's toils, lit up as he saw us. His lips, cracked and sore, smoothed into a huge great smile as we ran to greet him. Lizzie, the eldest always got to him first, and then me, who always stopped to help our little one-year-old sister, barely able to walk yet. He scooped us up; all three of us and I buried my nose against his neck to drink in the delicious oily sweaty smell of my daddy.

With one girl tucked under each arm and his immense hands tenderly holding little Eunice, he ducked under the doorframe to enter our home on Alfred Street just over the bridge by the lock on the canal.

We giggled with delight as he pretended to drop us, dipping down to greet our Ma; to kiss her, full on the lips before she scolded both him and us for getting our pinafores dirty with the foundry dust and grease that covered him.

"Jim, they're covered in dirt now!" she exclaimed in fake annoyance.

"I've had a hard day woman, hot, hard, and noisy!" he laughed, setting us down on the floor to wrap his sturdy arms around our Ma to spin her around.

We three little girls were the light in his life, a light stronger than any furnace fire, it burned within his heart until he was home again. Life, safely enveloped in those huge arms of our daddy, was safe and happy and we never dreamed it would end.

That one moment of complete warmth and happiness in an otherwise dour life, hard and toil weary, was the highlight of our day, our daddy was home safe, and we were surrounded by love.

I have few memories of him, just the happiness of his blue eyes, the way his hair curled at his collar and the recollection of his huge arms. To a little girl, my daddy was massive.

"Half an hour girls," commanded Ma. "Then it's bedtime."

On a Sunday, our days were filled with laughter. Daddy always laughed, his amusing tales and loud voice filling the room with happiness.

After Church, we would walk back home over the little hump-backed bridge and sometimes continue past our house, under the railway bridge and into Moston Brook, a quiet little wildlife habitat that seemed a world away from the hustle and bustle of life on the canal. All week barges fully laden with cotton bales would go through the

Alfred Street lock, going one way from the Liverpool ports through Manchester to the Pennines. Then they would return full of finished cotton fabric, timber, salt, and coal going back. Felt was brought down from Sowerby Bridge in Yorkshire, beyond the Saddleworth hills, along the canal to the Claremont Street hat factory.

Both Ma and Daddy would point out trees and birds along the way, Lizzie and I skipping along holding daddy's hand, him waving at the bargemen he knew as they opened the sluice gates to the lock and lead their horses along the towpath. Ma always trailing behind carrying little Eunice, helping her to pick little daisies and buttercups.

Our Ma's life was hard too, cleaning and washing, cooking, and looking after her little family. Our home was neat, but then we had very little in the way of furniture. Just a table and four hard wooden chairs, a pine dresser with a few plates and mugs neatly placed upon it; this was the room where we lived. In the corner on a smaller table sat a white enamel bowl and a huge earthenware jug for water, which had to be carried from the standpipe at the end of the row of 6 houses in Alfred Street, Failsworth. A pegged rug, homemade out of scraps of cloth lay in front of the large cast-iron range where our mother cooked in large pans above the fire and baked her bread in the oven set to the left-hand side of the fire. And then there was my favourite chair, a large pine rocking chair that Lizzie and I could sit on side by side. Daddy would make us squeal by pretending to sit down while we were there. He poised his huge frame over our laps and gently pretended to sit.

"This chair is lumpy Alice," he would say to Ma while Lizzie and I stifled squeals of delight. "I think you might need to sew me a cushion to sit on! This is rather odd, last time I sat down here the seat was smooth, now it's all bumpy!"

"Daddy, daddy it's us!" we shrieked, in fits of laughter.

"Well, I never!" he exclaimed laughing and scratching his head. "I didn't know little girls lived here! Who let them in Alice? Who let them sit on my chair?"

With hoots of laughter, we would both jump off and as soon as he sat down one or both of us would scramble back onto his knee, cuddling into his waistcoat while he coughed and tried to read his Sunday paper.

In the wintertime, aunts, uncles, and cousins would sometimes visit, the adults would drink tea and we children would play with shiny glass marbles or a spinning top. Some of my memories are very faint but the recollections of playing happily with cousins and the sound of polite adult conversation will remain with me always.

So too will my memory of the day they took my daddy away in a large wooden box.

Upstairs were two further rooms, our parents' large bed in one and another smaller room with a smaller bed for Lizzie and me. There was a chest of drawers in our parent's room and one small chest for our few belongings in ours. Another gaily coloured pegged rug lay on the floor at the end of our bed. Little Eunice occasionally slept top to toe with us but oftentimes she slept between ma and daddy lest she cried upon moving her once she was asleep. If we needed the toilet in the night, there was a large ceramic pot under the bottom of our bed. Daddy called it the 'gozunder' because it 'goes under' the bed. Such was his northern humour. In the morning our pot would be only half full but the one in daddy's room would be full, a disgusting mix of pee and blood from the constant coughing and spitting daddy did in it, and Ma had to take it to the privy to empty it.

Down the back of the row of houses was a row of tippler toilets for the entire street to use. The smell that permeated on a warm summer day was nauseous. Ma didn't like us to use the privy but as we grew older, this was unavoidable. We children played on the cobbles and our mothers gossiped at the doors as they did their chores.

This was life, we knew no different. It was Ma who told us many years later, just how bad it had been when we were small. As children we did not see that it was hard, overcrowding rife, dirt and disease a reality and many of our friends were ill. Countless thin and malnourished children died before they had the chance to grow. It was dirty and unsanitary, but it was all we had, all we knew and impossible to get away from no matter how hard our fathers worked. The local foundry employed daddy, as a spindle polisher and labourer, and the wages were better than in the cotton mills but were still poor enough to keep us locked into poverty.

Every night for the past few weeks' daddy would cough and cough almost all night, he would spit black blood into a grimy cloth and would lie shivering, soaked in sweat before he felt he could stand and manage the day's work ahead. Then, in the middle of a cold and bleak February, very early in the morning, so early that it was not true light, he leaned over to cough and spit and lay back down. Ma mopped his head with a damp cloth and then he was quiet.

So very, very quiet.

We waited.

It was too quiet. Lizzie jumped out of bed then, I wasn't far behind her, and we stood, barefoot in the doorway to their room. Ma glanced over to us, and her eyes met ours, stark and wide in the cold morning light.

She looked back down into the sleeping face of the man she loved, and her shoulders dropped. She wiped his face again and slowly breathed out, tears welling in her eyes.

A slow muffled wail came from out of nowhere and she fell forwards onto daddy's chest. Our beloved daddy was staring at the ceiling, his eyes fixed on nothing, his mouth open with a trickle of fresh blood slowly dribbling down his cheek and onto the pillow. I was beside the bed in an instance, and I started to cry.

"Daddy, daddy!" I begged, reaching out to touch the front of his cold, soaked nightshirt, but he couldn't hear me anymore.

There was a silence that I couldn't understand, only broken by the huge guttural sobs coming from my Ma. Lizzie held my hand as we stood by the bed, but I felt no warmth from it. She stood stock-still as if a soldier to attention and stared, open-mouthed straight into my face. I looked from her to my daddy and over to the sleeping child next to Ma, blissfully unaware of the fears unfolding.

After what seemed like an age, Ma sat back up, her face wet with salty tears and a look of fear on her face that I had never seen before. Her hand resting upon her rounded pregnant belly.

"Lizzie, go and fetch Mr Leslie. Be sharp".

Mr Leslie was a doctor, he was very well known on our street, and he certified all the deaths. My brave big sister, not yet six years old suddenly thrust into the grief of adulthood, hurriedly dressed, and ran out of the house and down the street with her shawl covering her head and shoulders. The rain, unsympathetic and cold lashing down on her as she went.

I remember standing at the window looking out, distractedly drawing lines in the condensation on the dirty glass. It was funny how it ran in dribbles from my fingers like the so many tears we had all shed that last couple of days. The heavy chenille curtains were closed behind me, blocking all light into the room. Not that there was much light that grimy winters day, and nothing to light up in that sad dreary little room. A few candles flickered, lighting the room sufficiently for the well-wishers to come and pay their last respects to my daddy.

"Beatrice, come away from the window at once," said ma as gently as she could, her voice croaky and distant. Everyone was quiet and hushed so as not to disturb the fragile stillness of the room.

I quickly wiped the steamed-up window with the back of my hand, rubbing it next down the front of my best Sunday dress, it was still too big for me, heavy and black; my white pinafore tied at the back with a black sash ribbon.

I had a black ribbon in my hair too.

"I hate it! I want to wear the blue one, daddy so likes blue." I sulked. I didn't like this, any of it. "Why is daddy so quiet?"

Eunice sat on Lizzie's knee quietly sucking her thumb. Poor little mite didn't know what was happening, what the day was about and what this would mean for us all. I wanted to scream and hear my daddy's laughter one more time, but how could he laugh in a big wooden box?

Lizzie said nothing.

They put the box with my daddy in into the back of a large horse-drawn black carriage. We followed, over the humpback bridge, the bargemen and women stood stark still, the men doffing their caps, heads bowed in mutual respect for yet another loss although there were so many. Everyone walked very slowly in the rain behind it in silence all the way to St John's Church. The words that the vicar said made no sense to Lizzie or me and as soon as that was over, we followed the black horses and the bier, further along to the cemetery.

There was a large hole, and the men slowly lowered the box with my daddy in down into it with a braided cord. The vicar said some other words, which made my poor ma gulp and sob uncontrollably onto her brother Joseph's shoulder. He handed her his black-edged handkerchief, and she wiped her red-rimmed eyes again.

"He's with our Elizabeth now, God rest her soul," Aunty Mary whispered.

"And his father, Bless them all." said someone else.

"Eye, The Good Lord gives, and he takes away." another voice joined.

"What will I do now, Mary?" sobbed Ma, to daddy's sister. "What is to become of us, I have a baby yet to be born and the little 'uns to feed."

Ma was sobbing loudly now as they shovelled dirt onto the box with my daddy in. I clung to ma's legs as Aunty Mary held her so that she wouldn't fall.

"Hush love, shhhh."

"The rent is due at the end of March and I've nowt left. I have some of it but with Jim being so ill, he's not had a lot of wages recently".

"Hush now Alice," Aunty Mary whispered. "Hush, we won't let you starve. We'll go to see the parish man tomorrow." Slowly they started to walk away from daddy, back down the path towards home. Lizzie followed behind looking pitiful, but I wouldn't let go of Ma.

It made little sense to me, but there was a deep feeling of uncertainty. For so long the earth had been solid under our feet, then it moved and now there was nothing but an emptiness.

Back at our house, there were sandwiches and little cakes prepared by a couple of our neighbours, who had looked after little Eunice while we were gone. The darkness had left the room and the big heavy drapes that had covered the window earlier this morning had been drawn back to let in the cold February light.

Now the table in the middle of the room was piled with food placed on little lace doilies and plates. Aunt Emily sat Ma down and handed her a plate with a couple of ham sandwiches on.

"Here you go Alice, eat up. You must be strong now," she whispered.

Lizzie and I looked hungrily over at the table but politely waited until the adults had all taken some food before taking a piece of bread each and a small cake.

They stood around talking more loudly now, sometimes a smile and a laugh as they all reminisced about my daddy, his sense of humour, his laughter, his hard work for his family and his love for us all were discussed in detail. It was all so final, so empty and the bread stuck in my throat as I tried to swallow back tears.

They were people I knew well, uncles, aunts and friends, but Daddy wasn't there to lift me onto his shoulders and feed me cake. I didn't want to look up at these people and I followed the lines of the floorboards, tracing the grain with my foot. Something caught my eye as I stared at the floor, by my feet was a little card, edged in black with some squiggly writing on it. I looked around guardedly; no one was looking at me. I picked up the little card and gently tucked it into the sash around my waist.

Later that night as we undressed for bed, Lizzie picked up the card as it fluttered to the floor when I untied my sash.

She started to read it, struggling with the words "In a.... a.... affect.... affectionate rem.... rememb...rance of James. The beloved husband of Alice Ann Humphreys. Who dep.... dep...arted this life Feb 17th, 1900, in his 33rd year and was this day in... int... interred at Failsworth cemetery. 5 Alfred Street Failsworth, Feb 22nd, 1900. With the family's kind regards.

"This is Daddy, Beatrice," she said, a glum expression on her face. "He's not here anymore.

Karol Darnell

Chapter two

Life without Daddy

I liked Aunt Emily. She was Daddy's favourite sister, younger by eight years. She was pretty and sang with a gentle lilting voice as she talked. Her hair was auburn and framed her face; she had curls that I liked to play with. She came into the house after knocking gently on the door and placed a large steaming pan onto the mat in the centre of the table. She lifted me and gave me a little kiss on the cheek. I wrapped my arms around her neck, my legs around her waist. She smelled lovely, of sweet biscuits mixed with fresh rain. I think I was her favourite too as she always picked me up first.

"Hiya! How' ya doin' Alice love?" she asked Ma in her sweet voice as she squeezed me and set me back down on my feet. I stood with my arms still wrapped around her leg and Eunice got up off the floor for her hug too. She stood with her little arms reaching up to her, and Aunt Emily obliged her.

"I've brought stew. A rabbit stew today girls, our George caught it, and we had carrots and a turnip in the ground out back. It's made enough for all of us."

"Thank you, Emily," answered Ma sniffling into a handkerchief. "I can't stop crying. I don't know what to do." She was sitting on the rocking chair in front of the meagre fire. We didn't have a lot of coal left in the coalhole or scuttle.

"I just don't know what to do." she repeated, looking quite miserable. Her hand on her round belly.

"Come on now, it's been a week, you have to be strong," Emily sang, putting a comforting hand on Ma's shoulder. "You must think about the girls now. We can't have you crying. Come on, we'll get through. The girls need you to be strong and we'll all help, I promise."

Just then there was a knock on the door. One of Daddy's friends popped his head around the door with a cheery grin.

"Can I come in?"

"Of course you can Joe, you're always welcome." Ma answered, dabbing her eyes in a vain attempt to cover that she had been crying.

"Come on in".

He stepped in and closed the door behind him. He took off his flat cap and shook his unruly hair.

"It's stopped rainin'." he stated. "But it's still cold out there, 'appen it might snow."

"Sit down Joe, make yourself at home." said Ma, nodding to one of the chairs near the table where Aunt Emily had placed the pan of rabbit stew. He sat down and smiled up at Aunt Emily and Ma, then down at Lizzie and me. He tousled the curls of little Eunice who was sitting near his feet now playing with a little wooden doll that used to be mine.

"I've got a penny each for you girls," he said to us, and Lizzie and I eagerly jumped up and down excitedly. Then we remembered our manners and stood still, upright with our hands by our sides in front of him.

"Oh Joe, you needn't," protested Ma. "But thank you very much. Say thank you to Mr Ward, girls."

We held out our hands and Eunice, finally on her feet, forgetting her dolly, copied us, standing with her tiny hand outstretched to receive her penny too.

"Thank you, Mr Ward." We replied in unison quickly sitting back down on the rug to examine our shiny new pennies. Lizzie watching Eunice that she didn't put it in her mouth.

Joe Ward was a platelayer on the railway. A hard and low paid job, out in all weathers checking the railway track.

The Hollinwood branch line of the Lancashire & Yorkshire railway from Manchester crossed the canal over a bridge a little way up from the lock at Wrigley Head and passed over another bridge quite near the end of the row of houses on our street. The railway line joined further up to the Middleton junction and Oldham branch line at Chadderton. Our daddy had worked in the foundry making plates and spindles for the railway among other industries and this is how the two men had met. They enjoyed each other's company and often walked home from work together. Sometimes they would share a drink of beer in the Bulls Head, The Anchor or another of the many public houses in Failsworth.

We knew Joe well and he was always kind to us, polite and well mannered. My daddy used to say Joe Ward was a gentleman and he certainly was a nice man to give us pennies from his hard-earned pay.

"You have beautiful children Alice Ann," Joe said. "Very sweet they are. I should like children one day too." He looked up at Aunt Emily and smiled. She blushed and instinctively tidied her hair with her fingers.

"Would you mind awfully if I called in to see you all occasionally?" he asked Ma.

"I said, you're always welcome Joe. There'll be another baby soon enough. I'd like it if you came to see us all." Ma answered, her faint smile genuine none the less.

Lizzie and I had stopped listening to the adults talking and were sitting cross-legged facing each other on the hearthrug playing pat-a-cake and trying to show Eunice how to hold her hands up to clap pat-a-cake with us. She very soon got bored and picked up her dolly again, holding it upside down and sucking on its foot.

Joe said he wouldn't stay long but he seemed to be lingering just a little. Then when Aunt Emily got up to leave, he said his goodbyes saying he would walk Emily home. They lived in opposite directions, she down Main Street with Grandma, not far from the hat factory and he lived with his Ma and Pa in a cottage on Wickentree Lane, not far from us.

"What a kind man," mused Ma as she placed the pan on the fire to warm through the rabbit stew. She had some bread leftover from yesterday that would have been our only food this evening if it weren't for the kindness of our grandma and daddy's family. She cut it into four small pieces and placed them on a small plate in the centre of the table. Then she dished out the stew between the dishes in front of us and we hungrily started to eat.

The stew tasted good, but Ma didn't eat much. She held her back with one hand and the other rubbing her round belly as if it hurt a little. She closed her eyes, breathing calmly through her nose and slowly back out again through pursed lips; She had been doing that for a few days now. She struggled to get up off the chair or out of bed and sometimes asked us to pull her arms so she could stand. We knew she was joking with us, and we tried and tried with all our might to pull her up, but always ended up tumbling backwards onto the floor laughing and giggling.

That night, earlier than usual she told Lizzie and me to take Eunice upstairs and to get her ready for bed. She kissed each of us in turn and I put my arms around her neck and kissed her too.

"Pop her in with you two girls will you please? Beatrice, help Lizzie, be good girls now. My back hurts".

Of course, we did as we were told. We were good children. We were just very sad now. There was a space; an emptiness, a silence in the house now that daddy wasn't here. Lizzie undressed Eunice and neatly folded her pinafore and dress placing them on the chest, leaving her shift on

under her nightshirt. She brushed her tousled
blond curls and formed ringlets around her fingers
like Ma usually did. She lay Eunice in the middle
of our bed and helped me also to get ready, helping
me to brush my hair too. Mine didn't have the curls
that Eunice's had so she brushed it straight and
tried to plait it, one on each side of my head. One
was higher than the other, but it was a very good
effort and far better than I could have done myself.
We climbed in between the cold sheets, one on
each side of our baby sister and cuddled up close
for warmth, all three lost in our own thoughts.

"Will Ma die too Lizzie?" I whispered. "She
said her back hurts. She might die though, might
she?"

"No, she won't leave us too Beatrice, she can't!
What would we do?" she whispered back.

I could see her breath in the cold room as she
spoke. I shivered despite the warmth of the baby
between us. Her little eyes were closed, and she
looked so pretty and innocent. I placed a tiny kiss
on her cheek and put my head back on the pillow,
staring at the ceiling.

"Ma has a baby in her belly Beatrice, she can't
die, who would take care of a baby and us?" she
murmured solving the problem in her own mind
at least. "We'd have to go to live with Grandma,
Aunt Emily, and the others. Or Uncle Joseph &
Auntie Jane in Manchester perhaps?"

"But babies die too Lizzie," I reasoned in a hushed voice. Firstly, so that I wouldn't disturb Eunice and secondly because I thought that if I said that out loud, it might come horribly true. Babies and mothers did die, many of them at the same time as each other. I couldn't bear that to happen, and a single tear dripped from under my eyelid.

The next day was a Sunday and Ma said she couldn't face Church and we weren't going. Grandma Humphreys called on her way home and Aunt Emily was with her.

"It seems to have stopped raining girls. Alice, could I take them for a little walk over the bridge and to look at the boats for half an hour?" Aunt Emily asked as we nodded our heads in excited agreement.

"Yes alright," answered Ma, "I'm sure the girls will like that." She turned to her mother-in-law of only nine years. "Will you stay here with me Elizabeth until they come back, please?"

"Of course, I'll pop the kettle on," answered Grandma as we hurriedly put on our clogs and shawls and went out of the door, eager to escape and to be able to run free.

"Stay on the path girls!" Aunt Emily shouted as we darted towards the brook. "This way, it's too muddy down there!"

Lizzie and I ran back towards her, no country walk today but at least we could feel the wind slap our faces. If I could run fast, I would run into the arms of my daddy once more.

We dashed ahead to stand on the brow of the little humpback bridge over the canal lock to wait for Aunt Emily and Eunice. She was splashing in puddles despite Aunt Emily telling her not to. Our bridge stood between Moston Brook and the mills of Failsworth on the opposite side. From here we could see our two worlds. The hustle and bustle of noisy life on the canal with the boisterous men on heavily laden barges contemplating the lock. The big wooden sluice gates that let the water in or out to carry the barges on to their destinations. The Ivy and Wrigley Head Mills with their large chimneys and constant clattering and whirring of the mill machinery inside. The cobbled towpath alongside the wall of the Ivy mill before the moorings where the barges would load and unload. The Springfield Works, where they made and washed cotton and silk cloths. A hive of industry that was fascinating to a child. The little stone steps down the side of the bridge with a worn old handle that the people would hold onto as they got on or off the barge, up to the towpath so that they could open or close the lock gates. The trees, standing tall and bare now in the grey afternoon smog of winter, and the little overflow weir that we called our secret waterfall. Lizzie said there were water nymphs and fairies who lived down there but Ma never allowed us to climb over to see if it were true.

Behind us was our little row of houses, dirty and black stoned - where once we were happy; beyond that and on the other side of the railway track, lay Moston Brook with trees and birds and wildflowers in the summertime. Now the winter trees were bare, their spindly branches reaching for the sky, wet, dank, and cold. They didn't hold out their arms to greet us as they used to do when Daddy was here. They stood, stark and desolate, waiting. Just waiting.

The busy life of the canal was in 'Sunday mode,' which wasn't too different to the working week when barges came and went through the lock constantly. The horses, their hooves clattering on the cobbles, being led by perhaps a raggedly dressed child, sometimes by the bargeman's wife while the men held the tiller of the wide and heavily laden barges as they manoeuvred through the lock and under the humpback bridge. But Sunday always seemed different somehow. Quieter. More reverent. Slower.

"Mornin!'" called one man from atop his barge as it rose in the water of the lock going uphill towards Rochdale. "Sorry to hear about your brother!" He doffed his cap and Aunt Emily smiled a thank you back to him. We didn't stay out long. We hurried back as it started to rain again.

"Come and dry off in front of the fire." said Grandma. "You'll catch your deaths!" She lifted Eunice and took off her shawl and hat and her muddy boots. "Another job for you Alice, boots to clean," she smiled, trying to lighten the mood placing them in front of the brass topped fireguard.

Aunt Emily didn't take her coat off. She and Grandma went home, leaving us alone in front of the fire, the only warmth on this cold wet day.

Ma sat on the rocking chair with a small cushion behind her. Eunice quickly fell asleep on her knee with the gentle rock, creak, rock, creak, rock of the chair like a lullaby. Lizzie was drawing a circle on her chalkboard with the number twelve at the top then numbers from one to eleven around the outside. It was a clock. She drew a line from the centre pointing straight up and another one pointing to the three.

"What time is it, Beatrice?"

"Three o'clock." I answered.

She rubbed out the line and drew one to point at the nine.

"What time is it, Beatrice?"

"Nine o'clock." I sighed.

She rubbed out the line again and drew one to point at the seven.

"What time is it, Beatrice?"

"Oh no!" I yawned, "seven o'clock."

"Well done. Now we will do half pasts." She rubbed out both lines and the whole routine started again.

"What time is it, Beatrice?"

"Stop it Lizzie, half-past four." I said inattentively.

After a while, bored with the lessons from Lizzie, I looked up and Ma was fast asleep too. She looked older than she had recently, but I loved her then more than I ever realised. Her face was peaceful. I nudged Lizzie, putting my finger to my lips.

"Shhhh!"

The only sound now was the crackle of the fire and the tick of the clock on the cupboard.

So peaceful.

Not deathly quiet like the day daddy died, but calm. Just quiet and soft, while we waited for our baby to be born.

Chapter three

Minnie

Some of the memories I have are my own, but oh, how they fade over time! Time can go so quickly, taking people away and showing us whom to love and reminding us that those two things are all that we truly have.

Time and love.

Memories are the constant ribbon that ties these two transient things together. Many of my early memories are from the stories Ma would tell us.

As children we would sit of an evening, on the floor, one of us with our head against her knee whilst she rocked on the rocking chair recounting tales of her own childhood.

"Tell us a story of when you were little Ma," begged Lizzie.

"When I was little," she said wistfully, grinning as her memories came flooding back. "I was born a long way away from here, in Coppenhall, Crewe. My father worked there as a railway engineer for a couple of years, but we didn't live there long, we moved back to Manchester when I was only two. My mother was from Cumbria and her father was a butcher. Then my mother died when I was four, my big brother Joseph was six and John was two. My mother was called Mary but that's all I remember about her really; and then my father married another lady called Janet Moss, a widow with three children and so there were six of us. My father and her had another baby but she died. She was called Janet too."

"What was your daddy called?" I asked.

"Josiah Smith Ellershaw," she announced as if he were a very important man. "He was the youngest of eight children of Betty and Joseph Ellershaw, a master bootmaker, and my father was a mechanic and machine fitter; a very lovely man."

"Do all daddies die?" I asked quietly.

"Not all of them, no. Just the best ones," she sighed smiling at me. "He was only forty-eight and he died of 'flu the year before I married your daddy. He made those two miniature brass tables, candle reflectors on the mantlepiece."

She gazed up at her most treasured possessions that her father had made when he worked at Steins in Hollinwood, and they sat in pride of place on her mantlepiece above the fire.

The glow from a candle placed in front of them was so warm and comforting, and she polished them with soot from the fire before rinsing them in soapy water once a week to make them shine.

She told us how she had started work at the age of twelve in the cotton mills; the long hard days, working as a card room hand.

"And then I fell in love with a fine and handsome man. We were so happy when you girls came along."

"Did we always live here, Ma? Is this where we were born?" asked Lizzie.

"No, you and Beatrice were born at 88 Church Lane, not far from St John's Church where we were married, and Eunice came along when we moved to 27 Alfred Street, below Oldham town. We had to move so daddy could work. Then we moved to this house in Alfred Street, near lock 65."

"This is the first home I remember," said Lizzie. "I don't remember anywhere else."

A small child remembers only minor snippets, yet the early experience of losing my daddy was vivid in my mind for many years. As a child growing up in the times that I did, death was always close. Death was all around, and I learned very quickly that the more I loved someone, the more likely they were to leave me. The more likely that death would be ever-present as I grew up, leaving me heartbroken each time that I trusted myself to try to love again.

I had kept the card with my daddy's name on it safe in a little cardboard box under my bed. It was all I had of him that was real. The smell of him, and the sound of his laughter. Those memories faded but that little card I could keep, helping me to remember him.

Over the years I would add many more cards to my box. Many happy memories too were kept within the cards in my box. Memories and people kept alive on little pieces of printed card.

But for now, in the early summertime of 1900, life was just about as sweet as it could ever be. We had a new little baby sister; Lizzie and I chose the name Minnie for her.

She had beautiful pale blue eyes set in a sweet petite round face. Her tiny nose was like a pearl and her ears, little seashells pink and perfect. A fuzz of blonde hair on her smooth round head. She had ten chubby fingers and ten flawless toes on her strong plump legs. Now that she was three months old, she was smiling at us and watching us play.

Occasionally one of us would lean into her cradle to kiss her or tickle her to make her giggle. We would blow raspberries on her soft skin and pretend to eat her fingers and toes.

Ma would sit on the rocking chair to feed her as we three played with our dolls, each pretending to be mothers ourselves, holding our babies to our breasts. At last, there was calm and happiness in our little world. Ma was completely besotted with her new baby and would rock her, crooning and whispering into her ear and kissing her beautiful head. Oh, we weren't jealous or upset at the attention Ma gave to Minnie, indeed she bestowed so much love and care to each of us.

When the baby slept each one of us all had attention off our Ma. Kisses, cuddles, guidance, and lessons. Ma thought it was very important that we girls were educated. She taught us our letters, our A, B, C's and how to write our names. Lizzie and I were good at counting and reciting our alphabet and we would, over the years test each other. I learned to recite my A B C backwards from Z Y X W.......

Eunice now slept in our bed with Lizzie and me. She was all grown up now that we had a new baby sister.

"You're a big sister too now," Lizzie told her.

"Minnie, she's my baby," she insisted. "I'm nearly three."

"My birthday's first, then Lizzie and then you will be three, after us." I told her in my grown-up 'I'm nearly four' attitude.

"Now girls, don't squabble!" ordered Ma. "It's Beatrice's birthday first. We might take a walk in the sunshine on Sunday. We might go on a picnic. Would you like that?"

Of course, we all excitedly agreed and at ten o'clock on that beautiful Sunday morning in June, we walked under the railway line and on through Moston Brook. This was usually how far we ever went but today Ma decreed that we would walk all the way to a secret place she knew called Boggart Hole Clough.

There was a big lake called a boating lake, a drinking fountain, and a promenade around the lake, she promised us. She told us that she used to go there with her father and brothers. She had asked Joe if he thought it might be too far for us to walk to, but he said he didn't think so and that he would accompany us in case we got lost or tired.

Joe was nice. He had kept to his word and had visited us often and always there were pennies, one for each of us girls. The one for Minnie he would give to Ma with a secret smile as he placed it in her hand and folded her fingers around it with his own.

On the day of our birthday walk, Lizzie, Eunice and I all skipped along holding hands while Ma and Joe pushed Minnie in a large black perambulator that she had borrowed for the day. She had packed some bread and cheese and some little buns that grandma had made. A large earthenware cask containing water was placed carefully near Minnie's feet in the pram and that was to be our picnic.

The day was dry and warm with just a touch of a breeze. I looked back over my shoulder, Joe was pushing the pram and Ma was walking like a fine lady with a black parasol resting on her shoulder and a black wide-brimmed hat with a beautiful feather plume upon it. We were in our Sunday best again but this time with our blue sashes around our waists and blue ribbons in our hair. Joe looked smart too in his Sunday suit and best collar with a silk tie at his neck. This was such a treat for us, poor as we were and yet the excitement was quite real, and we were not disappointed. The sun shone, we played on the grass, enjoyed our feast of a picnic, and walked completely around the boating lake watching the young boys sail their little sailboats, while the poorer children sailed their small pieces of wood that they dreamed were real boats.

We fell into bed that night tired but happy. He's not my daddy but he makes my Ma smile again. There is something about him that makes it feel all right. As if he's looking after us on behalf of daddy. Lizzie said she thought he liked Aunt

Emily, but he spends less time with her now and more with Ma and us.

Each of our birthdays that year passed with similar Sunday walks to somewhere nice, although it rained in July for Lizzies birthday and Grandma made a little afternoon tea for us all instead.

Little Minnie however was not happy. She seemed to be quite weak although she ate quite well. She cried a lot and couldn't settle, pulling her knees up to her chest in pain. She didn't seem to have any energy and wasn't growing as she should. Ma tried all she could to keep her comfortable and to help her sit up or crawl, but she didn't seem to be able to gather the strength.

Ma carried her about on a little cushion and nursed her most of the time, crooning and rocking her as she sat on the rocking chair.

Christmas came and went without much enthusiasm and before we knew it, our little Minnie was one year old. A great celebration and fuss was made of her but it was very clear to everyone that she was not very well. We couldn't afford a doctor for her and many a word of advice was given by Ma's friends and our family about what to do and how we might feed her well to strengthen her.

Ma thought it would be a good idea to move from our house as it was quite damp, noisy, and squalid. "Perhaps this is why Minnie isn't thriving?" I heard her say to Grandma.

"I've found you a house on Wrigley Head," said Joe one evening. "The rent is quite low but it's a bigger house with a front room, a kitchen and two bedrooms. It has a yard outside too and you won't have the noise from the railway and grime from the bargemen on the canal. I've given a guarantee from my pay to cover the rent."

"Oh, Joe love that's wonderful. I don't know how to thank you," Ma wept.

Lizzie and I were now at school and when we came home that afternoon our house was empty, the door standing wide open. I ran upstairs to where our bed had been to find there was nothing there!

Gone, all gone! Completely empty.

My box was not where I had carefully stored it. Panic welled up and I frantically ran back downstairs to where Grandma was waiting.

"My box!" I exclaimed bursting into tears. "My box, it's gone!"

"Of course, it has love," she said smiling at our worried faces. "Follow me. Your Ma has put your precious box in your new bedroom in your new house. Our George has been helping all afternoon! Say goodbye to the past girls."

The new house was very smart in comparison to the old one, with all the hustle and bustle and continuous noise. Wrigley Head was a street away from the canal and the mills. Our Uncle George had borrowed a handcart and all our worldly goods had been loaded onto it and transported to our new home. Aunt Emily had helped Ma with Minnie and Eunice. Someone else had given us some curtains, and although shabby and old, she helped Ma to hang them up.

There was a big front door with a number 42 on it made from metal. We had a front room with nothing in it, but it had its own fireplace. Ma promised that one day we would light a fire in there and have a sofa and dresser with some pretty ornaments on. She promised a rug, not a pegged one but a beautiful red woven one like Grandmas.

She promised that we would sit in our front parlour like proper ladies one day. She smiled at the dream and led us through another door. There was a back kitchen with room for our table and chairs, the rocking chair and our dresser with our crockery neatly stacked just as they were before. There was a fire in the range to cook on that was very similar but larger than the old one.

Outside was a backyard all our own too, here we could play, and Ma could hang out her washing. There was a tall wall around it and a back gate through which we could get to the privy down the backs.

In the room upstairs our bed was against one wall and another smaller bed stood along the opposite wall. Our clothes chest had been replaced with a tall set of drawers and a little nightstand for our candle and washbowl. This was a donation from our grandma. Lizzie and I threw our arms around her legs to hug her in thanks for this lovely gift.

A large window let in much more daylight than that of our old one and we could see over the backs of the houses of the two streets behind us on Clegg Street and Evening Street. We could see directly down the alley and over the walls of the back yards of all those houses. I was a queen surveying her new world.

"Lizzie is a big girl now," explained Ma. "She can sleep in this smaller bed and you, and Eunice can have the big bed together."

Lizzie squealed with delight and lay down on her 'new' bed.

"Ma where's my box?" I asked anxiously. "My box?" I was almost in tears at that point and my throat felt quite dry.

"Take a look. Where do you think I put it?" she quietly answered as she gestured towards the bed and walked out of the room. Of course, my box with my most precious card in it was there and all was well with my little world.

Downstairs again at suppertime, Minnie was crying quite a lot and she smelled too. Mother got her bowl and filled it with warm water from the kettle. She unwrapped her weak little baby and tenderly washed all the poo and blood away from her behind. She dressed her again in clean underclothes and tidied away the soiled ones putting them in a bucket of water outside in the yard. Then she held Minnie to her breast and fed her again. Feeding was the only thing that soothed Minnie and Ma was exhausted.

"Joe?" she asked as he sipped his tea. He had been a great help to us and a very good friend and confidant for Ma. "Would you approve if I spent the pennies you gave to Minnie? I have a mind to take her to the doctor."

"Goodness me Alice I wouldn't mind at all," he replied. "We can't go on like this, poor mite. I'll try to get some more overtime to help."

"Oh Joe, you're so kind," she said, choking on tears. "I'm at a loss. I can't feed my children. I have so little money. If Minnie were well, I could go back into the mill and work myself to feed them."

Joe put his hand on her shoulder as she rocked her baby, her eyes full of un-shed tears.

Chapter four

The Doctor

When Lizzie and I came in from playing one afternoon about a week later, Ma was telling Grandma about her day and her visit to the doctor. We were told to go upstairs and play but Lizzie and I had made listening to adult conversation an art. It was fun and secret, and so we took turns to creep halfway down the stairs to listen in to the muffled conversation coming from the kitchen.

"I caught the Manchester tram," Ma said, her voice quite strong.

"You went to Monsal?" asked Grandma, her voice quieter and further away.

"Yes, they treat infectious diseases. They were so rude to me! They said I might like to see the charity doctor!" continued Ma. "Well, I told them I could pay for treatment…she changed her tone a little then and directed me to his office."

"So that's how you found Doctor George Beattie?"

"Yes, he's Scottish. It was a nice place, a white painted house with three stone steps up to a large solid wooden front door. I rang the large brass bell and the door opened. A young girl in a dark dress with a white apron and stiff little nurse's cap on her head beckoned me inside."

Grandma mumbled something that I couldn't quite hear, Lizzie and I exchanged a shrug, she placed her finger over her lips and crept down a couple more steps.

Ma continued speaking and I joined Lizzie two more steps down so that I could hear.

"...told me to take a seat and asked me my name. I was so nervous."

Minnie started to wail, covering up what Ma said next, but it sounded like a description of the room "...dark and cold ... small window next to the door and another internal door to the right... dark and panelled with dark wood halfway up the wall... very cool."

Minnie squealed and whimpered.

"Here, let me take her, shhhhh child, there, there." Minnie was clearly uncomfortable as grandma tried to soothe her.

"Fireplace... panelled over... cream painted plaster patterned with swirls... smelled... heavy smell of pipe tobacco smoke…she fell asleep on my knee."

Minnie quieted, whimpering a little and we could hear Ma again,

"On another chair opposite me was a lady dressed rather finely with an air about her, unfriendly and aloof. She held her head in such a way, I'm sure she was looking down her nose at me."

"You shouldn't feel less because you're poor Alice, your child is just as important as she is. Always hold your head high love," advised Grandma.

"Well, then the little internal door opened, and the nurse called me through."

"What was he like?"

"He was an older grey-haired man with a square set jaw in a rugged, yet kind face. He wore a smart tweed suit with a silk cravat around his neck and a pipe held between his teeth. As I entered the room a cloud of smoke wafted towards the open doorway behind me. He told me to take a seat and asked what the problem was. I told him the troubles that Minnie had and how she seemed to be very weak and in pain so much of the time. How she couldn't stop soiling herself, and how there was blood every time she did. After a few more considered puffs, he slowly took his pipe out from between his teeth and took out the pocket watch on a chain from his waistcoat pocket."

"Then what did he say?"

"Och, I don't think this one will live!" repeated Ma in a fake Scottish accent. "Then he told me to lie her on the couch so he could examine her. He rolled up Minnie's dress, he was very gentle as he felt her little stomach."

"Was Minnie alright with all that prodding? asked grandma, full of questions as she shushed the whimpering baby in her arms. From where her voice was coming from, I thought she was near the fireplace. Lizzie and I were almost at the bottom of the stairs now, straining to hear their muffled voices.

"He placed two fingers on her little chest and tapped them with the fingers of his other hand then listened to the hollow sound it made. He told the nurse to remove her undergarments so that he could inspect the bloody and soiled mess. Then he gently replaced her dress to cover her and took a long considered drag on his pipe. Then he said "Hmmm! As I thought, Mrs Humphreys. This wee child is quite sick."

"What did he say it was?"

"He said she has tuberculosis of the intestines. An ulcerated colon. Oh Elizabeth! He said nothing could be done." Ma started to cry, and grandma became quiet too.

"He said… he said…children die every day… he said…I can advise you love her and feed her well. But she will not thrive. I'm very sorry… That's all he said," Ma wailed louder now.

That was it, the catapult into the truth for me and Lizzie. The firing gun that propelled us forwards, and within seconds we had burst through the door at the bottom of the stairs and were in floods of tears too, hugging our Ma and kissing little Minnie. The four of us were bereft, only darling little Minnie was quiet, wondering what all the tears were for. Eunice, watched us from her seat on the floor, sucking her thumb in blissful ignorance.

"Go and play outside girls," said Grandma quietly through her tears after a good ten minutes. She handed Minnie back to Ma. "I think your Ma needs to change and feed Minnie. Run along you two, we'll get by. We'll be alright, I'm sure."

She firmly shooed us outside, bending to pick Eunice up to wipe her nose on the corner of her apron. Grandma was always enthusiastic, which instantly quelled any worries that we small children might have. Her positive and happy nature made us feel a little better and we reluctantly went outside.

Looking back now I realise that adults had a way of doing that; and we innocently believed that, just because she had told us things would be alright, they would be and yet again we believed her.

And so that afternoon, I stood on our front doorstep watching Lizzie skipping in the street with a piece of rope; she was counting how many she could skip.

I looked past her and along the street, Joe was returning from work. He always came to our house now on his way home and came in to see how we were most days. Today was no different and we followed Joe back inside to our back room where Ma repeated much of her story of the day's events to him.

Grandma said she would put the kettle on and see what was in the pantry for tea. She scooped up Eunice again and, grabbed my hand to usher us back out of the room, but by this time she realised that even though we were too young to perhaps hear the horrible news, we did in fact understand and knew it all already.

Eunice squealed and wriggled free, running back to Ma where she flung herself into her skirts and wouldn't let go.

It was all a little chaotic with Ma crying, and all the questions from Joe. Lizzie and I stood hand in hand listening to it all over again how we might lose our sweet baby sister.

Some days it seemed that time passed very slowly since Ma's visit to the doctor, and sometimes it passed far too quickly. Somehow, we managed to carry on with life as it was. We still made Minnie smile as we played. We continued to play with her and helped her to learn to use a spoon. She made us laugh when she banged her spoon onto her dish, spraying her porridge over us. She always ended up with food in her hair, but it didn't seem to matter at all. She was weak but a happy child for the most part. Sometimes she would scream with pain and was very poorly and Ma realised that some foods made her pain worse, so she gave her the best food that she could out of our scant supplies.

We went again one day that warm summer, to Boggart Hole Clough for another picnic like we had the year before. We were all another year older and more observant of the world around us.

This time I realised that there was so much more to see, so many more trees, plants and flowers. Vast ancient woodland with soft green undergrowth that stretched away down the hillsides as far away as we could imagine. Craggy gullies and dark rocky places falling away from us as we looked down from the bridge near the lake. There was a stream at the bottom of a huge valley, with ferns and verdant green foliage tumbling over large rocks. Shrubberies of dog roses and rhododendron, bluebells and poppies; Trees of many different types and sizes, some with dark knobbly bark and some with silvery trunks that reached high up to the sky.

"Is that where the Boggart might live Joe?" I questioned, a little afraid as we looked down from a bridge into a gully below.

Joe smiled down at me. "The Boggart might be on his holidays at this time of year, I don't think he is likely to spring out and gobble us up!" He took hold of my hand. "Although we must be careful because I might be wrong," he added with a mischievous cackle, his eyes wide and playful with a huge smile that reminded me of my daddy. I smiled up at him and he squeezed my hand as if he knew.

Gliding gracefully along on the lake were three beautiful white swans and little ducks with their yellow ducklings swimming away from us; coots with white head feathers and moorhens among the reeds. Pigeons were pecking about for seed on the path. Large, black-necked Canadian geese with their fluffy brown goslings and their funny honking noises gathered around us pecking on the ground to collect grass and little leaves. A few of them pecking each other and fighting over the smallest sprig or piece of greenery.

We all laughed when their babies followed them making little peeping noises copying their parents.

We stood together silently and watched in amazement as a young grey heron poised motionless on a log among the reeds not very far from us. He stood stock-still among the yellow water iris watching patiently until gracefully and swiftly he suddenly dived into the water, beak first like a javelin to triumphantly rise with a small wriggly fish.

He lifted his head and swallowed the little fish whole.

"Gosh, that's fabulous!" exclaimed Lizzie, clapping her hands together. "Ma, did you see?"

"Do it again, Mr Heron please," pleaded Eunice, jumping up and down in excitement.

"He can't do it again Eunice. That's his dinner. Isn't he clever?" answered Lizzie.

This time after we walked around the boating lake we continued through the woodland and down a very steep hill. Joe panted and puffed pushing the pram back up the hill on our way back and he said that he must be getting old. Ma laughed like a schoolgirl and joined him, side by side pushing Minnie up the hill in the huge black pram with a sleeping Minnie safe inside.

We got back to Failsworth at half-past five; we walked past our old house and over our hump-backed canal bridge, waving to the canal people. Away from the canal and onto Wrigley head where we now lived: Further yet again, along the street, past our new house, continuing up Wickentree Lane where the houses were slightly nicer, with little walls outside the front and clean neat flagstone paths leading to steps up to the front doors.

We stopped outside number 57. A white painted, double fronted cottage set back from the road, with gardens in front, a neat little path, and a workshop to the side. Ma straightened her skirts and her hat.

She wet her fingers on her tongue and patted our hair with nervous fingers, smoothing it in an attempt to make us look presentable. When she was happy with our appearance, as tatty and poor as we were, she nodded to Joe to open the door.

We had been invited to tea with Joe's Ma and Pa. We were instructed to be polite and mind our manners. Speak when we were spoken to and NOT misbehave.

"At all!" Ma stated firmly holding up her finger to each one of us to exaggerate that she really meant it.

She followed Joe inside carrying Minnie on her cushion, leaving the pram outside. Lizzie cautiously followed, then Eunice and me last. We each clasped our hands in front of us as we entered the front room. Here was a very different room to our front room. There was a beautifully polished table with chairs to match. A dark wood dresser full of pretty plates and ornaments stood in one alcove next to the chimney breast. Ceramic animals and birds were placed on another sideboard with a huge mirror in the centre. Stood in front of the large, tiled fireplace was a fat ceramic plant pot with a parlour palm in it and a huge aspidistra on a low table with barley twist legs was placed in front of the window. Heavy chenille drapes hung there, tied back with cords. To the side of the fireplace in the other alcove was a piano. I was awestruck.

"Come on in everyone, make yourselves at home," welcomed Mrs Ward, beckoning us all forwards.

"Mrs Ward, may I introduce my daughters. Beatrice, Eunice, and Elizabeth Alice." Ma introduced us as we each politely stepped forwards.

"Sarah, please. Call me Sarah." Mrs Ward said to Ma. "This is my husband, Henry."

Joe's father stepped forward and shook Ma by her hand. "A pleasure to meet you, love," he said, smiling at Ma putting her instantly at her ease. "This must be little Minnie." He gently touched her cheek with the back of his finger.

Introductions made, we were invited to sit down while Mrs Ward and Joe fetched the plates from the back kitchen. Ham and tomato sandwiches and some little cubes of cheese. Slices of cucumber and a big dish of a homemade pickle.

Then there was a plate with slices of cake and biscuits on it.

A large pitcher with ginger beer in it was for us three and a small ale for each of the adults.

It was a perfect end to a perfect day. Mr and Mrs Ward were very nice people and we left there that Sunday evening in the middle of June feeling fed well, totally at home and completely happy.

Sadly, that happiness would only last until the end of that summer.

On a warm and clear October morning after only a year and seven months of life, our darling Minnie passed away.

We laid my poor unfortunate baby sister to rest under a weeping willow tree, a step or two away from the daddy she never knew and who never met his little girl. A daddy we all loved so dearly and lost, just as we had loved and lost our pretty little Minnie. I clung to that little card with my sister's name printed upon it, until I could take it upstairs to place it with my Daddy's card in my box.

Chapter five

A Christmas

dinner

We stood Minnie's photograph on our mantelshelf above the fireplace, and we all whispered goodnight to her in our prayers every night. Her photograph was taken so that we could remember her pretty face and keep her in our thoughts even though she was now gone.

Even now I can see her face when I close my eyes, I can still remember the day she was born and her smile as she watched us play. Although she had been weak, I felt her willingness to live and be one of us and I will hold this in my heart. Looking at the photograph of my dead baby sister comforted us all and helped us to recall her curls, her soft skin on her chubby little face. Keeping her alive and helping us to bear the pain of her parting.

"Why did Minnie have to die?" questioned Eunice. "She was my baby sister and I loved her." Ma took Eunice onto her knee and rocked her gently, both of them saying nothing for a long time.

"She was very ill love. No one could make her better," said Ma with a broken, sad voice. "The doctor said that nothing could be done and all we could do is love her. I suppose we will never forget her, poor mite."

"Will I die too Ma?" Eunice asked.

"Goodness me no, not for a very long time I hope!" replied Ma, holding her now youngest daughter closely to her.

Eunice buried her face in Ma's chest and sobbed. "I don't want to die Ma. I'm so very frightened."

"Hush child. Don't speak like that. We must all love each other and be kind and look after each other. No one else will die, I promise."

Ma's heart was truly broken, and tears flowed down her face, dripping onto Eunice's head.

I heard my mother's promises with a child's trusting belief and yet a wary mind. Who would have ever been able to promise that first Daddy and now Minnie would have ever left us to cry at their loss?

"Oh, Ma!" cried Lizzie. "I hurt with how much I loved Minnie. Sweet little Minnie," she collapsed to her knees and threw her arms around ma's legs; she buried her face in her skirts.

I couldn't utter a single word. I simply sobbed, falling next to Lizzie and hugged my dear Ma and sisters.

We were all subdued for the next few weeks. The house was quiet, and we tried to be as gentle as we could be with Ma, but sadness was always there. Minnie had captured everyone's hearts and there was yet again emptiness in our lives.

Joe was so kind and many evenings he would hold Ma, stood in front of the fire, while she silently cried. Cradling her in his arms and stroking her hair. When he looked up it was obvious that he had cried too.

One Sunday afternoon, shortly after we had lost Minnie, Lizzie had gone with Eunice to visit Grandma. It was cold outside, but it had stopped raining at least. I felt unwell and just wanted to stay in front of the fire and keep warm. I sat quietly playing with my doll on the rocking chair with a knitted blanket spread over my knees and a large handkerchief that I snuffled into from time to time.

Joe was comforting Ma, just holding her while they stood in front of the fire as it crackled in the grate. I suppose they had forgotten that I was there as I was so quiet. I looked up and saw them swaying together as if to some gentle music only they could hear. Ma lifted her head from off his chest. He placed his first finger gently under her chin and lifted her face to his. She smiled very slightly, and he dipped his face to hers to softly kiss her on the lips. She didn't move away, she stayed there in his arms, and he kissed her tenderly once again. Then he smiled lovingly down into her face, and she smiled back at him.

I carried on playing with my doll and said nothing. It was so normal, so gentle, and so calm.

Christmas dinner that year was a very special one. We were once again invited to Joe's parents' house. Joe said that his two youngest sisters, Nancy and Annie would be there, and they were eager to meet us all. Joe was one of nine children, three brothers and five sisters.

That morning, Ma had said that she felt a little sick but was now feeling better. We set off just as it started to snow, tiny flakes landing softly on the cobblestones as we trouped along Wrigley Head towards Wickentree Lane.

We arrived at two o'clock and Mrs Ward welcomed Ma with a smile and a warm embrace.

"Come in, come in, Merry Christmas." Mr Ward welcomed cheerily. "How lovely to see you all."

"Henry, their coats." Mrs Ward instructed. "Merry Christmas girls."

We all wished each other a Merry Christmas as we shook the light snow off our shawls and hair. We entered the front room to see the fireplace festooned with a garland of red-berried holly and ivy that Joe had picked from the railway embankment. A small Christmas tree stood in the corner and was decorated with shiny little ornaments and pretty ribbons. Nancy and Annie stood side by side by the fireplace and both smiled kindly at us as we entered the warm room. Nancy had copper coloured hair that shone as it reflected the light from gas lamps and the many candles that were placed around the room. Annie, smaller than her sister had a fair complexion and her hair was lighter in colour.

Before us stood a large oval table which was set with a beautiful white tablecloth and two huge brass candelabra with three tall candles in each. Mrs Ward and the two girls disappeared through a door to the left and when she reappeared, she was carrying an enormous plate with a huge piece of roast beef on it. The girls walked behind her with more serving dishes. There were roasted potatoes heaped onto a plate, carrots, parsnips, and sprouts in another big bowl. A large jug of steaming gravy stood next to the beef.

The sight and aroma filled our senses as if we had never encountered food before. We eagerly sat down and the biggest Christmas dinner that we had ever faced in our young lives commenced.

Mr Ward made a great ceremony of carving the joint, placing the slices on a side plate. Nancy helped Eunice and me to place some meat on our plates and then she handed me the dish of potatoes and a large spoon. Rather shy and unaccustomed to meals like this, I almost reached out with my hand to grab the food; I caught a look from Ma, lifted the spoon and carefully placed two on my plate and two on Eunice's plate.

Minding the manners that our dear Ma had taught us; we devoured our meal as graciously as we could possibly manage. The meat was delicious and needed little chewing. Crunchy crisp roast potatoes with soft fluffy centres, and the homely taste of mashed turnip; carrots cooked in butter, roast parsnips and sprouts cooked to perfection with tiny pieces of crispy bacon.

"Would you like more gravy? asked Annie and I eagerly nodded my head, my mouth so full I couldn't speak.

"Goodness, that was delicious Sarah. Thank you. I'm very full now." Said Ma to Mrs Ward. "Girls?" she added nodding to us in expectation of our thanks.

"Thank you for a wonderful dinner, Mrs Ward." Lizzie said politely. Eunice and I repeated her very words as we were dumbstruck as to how else to say how tasty that meal had been.

Mrs Ward smiled proudly and started to tidy up the plates, nodding to Annie who took them through to the back room.

"It's so lovely to have you all here." she answered.

Mr Ward winked at me as he followed his youngest daughter out of the room; he then reappeared with a large plate of figgy pudding, aflame!

We all gasped in awe at the sight. We had never seen such a festive spectacle. He placed the pudding down in the centre of the table just in front of me and winked at me again.

"I wonder if you're too full for some pudding?" he asked playfully.

I nodded quickly with my eyes and mouth wide open.

"Beatrice!" Ma whispered and shook her head at my bad manners, but that only served to make Mr Ward laugh even louder and put us all so much more at ease.

"I shall serve this pretty lady first." he said to Ma and we three girls all started to giggle.

Pudding devoured, Joe awkwardly stood up, cleared his throat, and raised his glass of port.

"Merry Christmas," he started. "Thank you, Alice Ann, girls… for joining us for this special day. Thank you, Ma and Pa, for providing this delicious food." He cleared his throat again, placing his glass back down on the table and, very nervously walked around the table and took Ma's hands in his.

"Alice Ann, I wondered if you would marry me and be my wife?"

There was a hush as everyone held their breaths. We were all taken aback, but Ma the most of course. She sat staring up at him without saying a word for quite a long while, a look of surprise and relief across her face, which turned into a beautiful smile as she caught Joe's gaze.

"Joe." She stuttered shaking her head in disbelief. "Oh, Joe! Yes. Yes, I will!" She stood up and threw her arms around him.

The table erupted in a riot of noise. Lizzie and I squealed, Mr Ward shouted, "Congratulations Son! and to you Alice Ann!" raising his glass too; first looking at Joe and then Ma.

Mrs Ward, as taken aback as we all were and staring agape at her husband, slowly closed her mouth and broke into a huge smile.

Nancy, Annie, Lizzie, Eunice, and I all clapped our hands and hugged each other as Mr Ward stood to walk around the table. He shook Joe's hand and embraced Ma. Mrs Ward kissed both Joe and Ma in turn and then each of us.

"Of course, it might not be for a while, Alice has found employment in the mill again and I've been promoted to foreman platelayer. We need to get together some money, perhaps it will be in the spring." Joe was telling his Ma.

My sisters and I had stopped listening to the adults, as we were too busy holding hands, dancing around them both in a circle with hoots of happiness.

When the rejoicing subsided and the table had been cleared, Mrs Ward sat down at the piano and ceremoniously lifted the polished lid. She adjusted her piece of music in front of her, gently stroked the piano keys and sat up straight. She spread out her fingers and placed them on certain keys, gently pressing each one as a most beautiful chord of music filled the room. As she started to play Mr Ward cleared his throat and stood next to his wife facing us and began to sing.

> *"When first I saw the love light in your eyes,*
> *And heard your voice like sweetest melody,*
> *These words of love to my enraptured soul,*
> *The world has not but joy in store for me.*
> *I love you as I've never loved before,*
> *Since first I saw you on the village green,*
> *Come to me 'ere my dreams of love are o'er,*
> *I love you as I loved you,*

When you were sweet
When you were sweet sixteen."

We all clapped as Mr Ward took a bow, turning to Mrs Ward he kissed her hand.

"Me, Me!" Said Eunice to our surprise; she stood up turning round to face us all. She waited until there was a complete hush in the room and then her sweet voice sang out.

> *"Away in a manger, no crib for his bed,*
> *The little Lord Jesus lay down his wee head.*
> *The stars in the heavens looked down where he lay,*
> *The little Lord Jesus asleep in the hay.*
> *The cattle are lowing, the poor baby wakes,*
> *But little Lord Jesus, no crying he makes.*
> *I love thee, Lord Jesus! look down from on high,*
> *And stay by my cradle till morning is nigh.*
> *Be near me, Lord Jesus; I ask thee to stay*
> *Close by me forever and love me I pray.*
> *Bless all the dear children in thy tender care,*
> *And fit us for heaven to live with thee there."*

Her voice was clear and sweet and rang out like a perfect bell. We all clapped our hands in appreciation of her bravery and effort and Mrs Ward said Eunice had the voice of an angel. The purest voice she had ever heard, she said.

She also promised that she would teach me how to play the piano, so enraptured was I with the thought of the beautiful music that could be made by touching those ivory keys.

Eventually, after many more songs and piano playing, and a poem recited by Nancy, our most wonderful Christmas day evening was over. Ma and Joe held hands as we walked back home. The light snow had now stopped and turned to light misty rain. We were all quite damp as we entered our cold back room, which brought us all back down to earth rather rapidly.

Joe took the coalscuttle out to fill it with coal, bringing it back only half full.

"There's not enough to fill it," he stated with a sigh. "I'll get some from home tomorrow."

He placed a few pieces on the dying embers waiting until they smouldered enough to gain enough heat to burn. Finally lit, he threw the rest of the coal onto the fire.

By the time he had managed to get the fire burning again, Eunice had climbed onto the rocking chair and looked at him intently.

"If you marry my Ma," she mused, "you can be my daddy and this rocking chair will be yours."

He smiled lovingly at her rubbing his dirty hands down the front of his best waistcoat. He lifted her from the chair and sat down, taking her onto his knee and started to rock backwards and forwards with little Eunice happily snuggling into him as he rocked.

Life got back to normal very quickly after that wonderful Christmas day. Ma started to work in the mill again; we went back to school, and Eunice spent each day at grandma's house. Every day after school Lizzie and I were instructed to go straight to Grandma's house on Main Street. It wasn't very far, and we were ordered not to dawdle, but Lizzie had so many friends, we were almost always late. One day a group of boys started to follow us, taunting us and pulling the plaits that hung down our backs. I started to cry, and Lizzie was very cross with them, she turned around with a furious face and pulled out her tongue at them! They laughed and taunted her more; so, outraged, she growled at them and started to chase after them, all the way back down Pole Lane, her long plaits flying out behind her. By the time she ran back to me, I was laughing so hard to think that she could scare a group of boys.

"It's not fair!" she exclaimed. "How dare they pull our hair and upset my little sister!" Indignant and always so protective of me. She grabbed my hand, and we skipped home to grandma's house together.

Grandma, Aunt Emily, and the rest of the family were completely ecstatic to hear the news of the wedding. Grandma fussed and planned new dresses for us three girls. She said we needed to be on our best behaviour.

"...and flowers, what about flowers? There's a cake to be made; have they spoken to the vicar?"

We all allowed the excitement to catch us up and carry us along and two weeks after Easter on 12th April 1902, my beautiful Ma walked down the aisle at St John's the Evangelist Church in Failsworth for the second time in her thirty-five years, as a bride again. She walked slowly, almost reverently to sweet organ music, arm in arm with her elder brother, our Uncle Joseph. My sisters and I carrying posies of flowers followed close behind her until we stopped where Joe stood near the altar waiting for her. He smiled nervously as she approached him, then she turned to hand her posy of flowers to Lizzie.

She turned back to Joe and the vicar, and we took our seats on the front pew next to Grandma, Aunt Emily and the others.

"Doesn't she look beautiful?" whispered Grandma to us, then putting her finger to her lips. "Shhhh." The church fell silent as the organist stopped playing and the vicar started to speak.

"Dearly beloved. We are gathered here today..." his booming voice loud and strong in the hushed church.

Karol Darnell

Chapter six

Joe

I sat on the hard Church pew that happy day, swinging my legs and watching the pink ribbons on my new dress shimmer in the ray of dappled sunlight that came through the stained-glass window above the altar.

Grandma had worked very hard over the past few weeks sewing new dresses for the three of us out of an old dress of hers. She had gone each Saturday to the market at the end of Wrigley Head to buy scraps of lace and pretty pink ribbons to sew onto them for our Ma's wedding to Joe. Each dress was adorned with pink ribbons and lace so that they matched each other, yet each one was slightly different. Eunice's' had more lace, Lizzies more ribbon, and mine a little of both.

Grandma had transformed me into a princess and my dress was exquisite. Last night she had bathed us in a tin bath in front of the fire and washed our hair, wrapping it in rags to curl it; then this morning she had tied our hair with pretty ribbons to match our dresses and we each held a posy of white roses and lily of the valley tied with the same matching ribbon.

If I were a princess that day, then my Ma was the most radiant queen I could ever imagine. Her dress was borrowed and quite simple in design, but she had added extra lace to match the lace on ours. She wore a veil of lace too which Joe had lifted from her face as she stood by his side, and they exchanged smiles.

Occasionally we had to stand to sing the hymns, the deep mellowness of Mr Ward's voice from the opposite pews and Eunice's crystal-clear voice beside me, filling the church with a most beautiful sound that I never wanted it all to end.

Finally, the service was over, and I now had a new daddy, a Grandpa Ward, and a Granny Ward. We followed Ma and Joe out of the church, out into the weak April sunshine that followed the snow earlier in the month. Everyone was happily shaking hands and exchanging kisses, talking and smiling.

Many people in Failsworth knew each other and Grandma had known Mr & Mrs Ward for a long time, ever since the Humphreys family had moved to Failsworth from Trefonen near

Oswestry in Wales, years before. I once asked her where it was and she said it was a very long way from Failsworth but there were pretty hills and valleys and quaint little cottages, but no work and so they had to move north. She told me that was why Aunt Emily sang so beautifully and that little Eunice had inherited her singing voice from her and our daddy.

That evening I hadn't wanted to take my princess dress off, but Eunice absolutely refused to. So, Ma sat on the rocking chair with Eunice on her knee until she had fallen asleep, her pretty ringlets across her face. Then Joe gently lifted the sleeping child and Ma skilfully took off the dress. Joe then carried Eunice to her bed. I then decided that I would take off my dress, as I didn't want to spoil it and I didn't need to be carried to bed in my underclothes!

I scurried upstairs and had to carefully climb around the sleeping Eunice to the opposite side of the bed, but I couldn't sleep. I lay awake reminiscing on the day's happy events.

The night was cool, and I could tell that Lizzie was awake in her own bed too.

"Lizzie," I whispered. "Pssst!"

"Yes?"

"I can't sleep, I'm so happy" I sighed.

"Me too. Wasn't it a fabulous day? I don't think I've ever been so… so… contented," Lizzie stated, yawning. "I wonder if Ma and Joe, I mean Pa will have children now that they're married?"

"I suppose they might." I pondered. "Another little girl to replace Minnie. Or lots of little girls, lots and lots of girls. Boys are horrid, aren't they?"

"Who was the man next to Joe in Church?" she asked.

"Pa, you mean." I giggled now we had to call Joe, Pa. "I think he was his friend. His name was Joe too I think."

"Oh yes, Joe Taylor and his wife Ellen. I remember him now. I've seen them in Church before."

"We have two grandmas now." I yawned and stretched, trying to once again find that warm spot in my bed.

"Mmmmm." agreed Lizzie.

"Girls, be quiet and go to sleep," came the whispered command from Ma as she peeked around the bedroom door. If she expected Lizzie and me to be quiet after such a wonderful day, she had misread us. She smiled as she crept into our room, avoiding the creaky floorboard. She leaned over Lizzie, gently stroking her eldest daughter's hair and cheek with her long slim fingers.

"Happy?" she asked.

"Oh yes, Ma," Lizzie replied. "You were a beautiful bride and Joe, so handsome."

"You'll be a beautiful bride too one day." She said as she leaned down to kiss Lizzie. "Goodnight, God Bless."

I had stood up in readiness and flung my arms around Ma's neck. My cheek touching her cheek as she wrapped her arms around me too and held me to her.

"Be careful, you'll wake Eunice," she cautioned as she moved her face to kiss me. "Lie down now and go to sleep."

I did as I was told, and Ma leaned over to pull the blanket around my shoulders. She looked down at Eunice and gently put a finger to her lips, placing it then on Eunice's forehead.

"Goodnight my pretty girls," she whispered as she left the room.

The last thing I heard before falling into a deep sleep, was the creak of bedsprings as she climbed wearily into her own bed next to her new husband.

Not only did we have a new daddy and a whole new family, but we also learned quite soon after that we were indeed to have a new baby too!

"I knew you would, I knew you would," I shouted, jumping up and down with the thrill of the news.

"Well, we are!" Said Ma resigned to the fact. "I'm going to need you girls to help me. You're much bigger now than when our Minnie was born and that was all very sad, but I think you might like to help me to clean, do the washing and cook some food so that you can all help Pa when the time comes and when our baby is small. Lizzie, you will have to help me to wash the clothes. You're nearly eight now and big enough to fetch water for me and help."

"Me, me." I interrupted. "I can help."

"Of course, you can. I will need you to help Eunice to get dressed and keep her entertained. I can't run after you three and look after a house, husband and new baby. You can also learn to prepare some food and keep the place tidy."

"I always help," said Lizzie pouting. "I swept the floor last weekend."

"I had to ask you three times, Lizzie and you sulked about it. I need you all to just accept that the work needs to be done and we women must do it," she said wearily. "Pa will need his tea when he comes in from work and he will want a tidy house."

"I will help too," promised Eunice earnestly and we all agreed that we would help, and we promised not to sulk or argue about it. Ma told us that we had to learn to look after Pa as we would one day be wives ourselves and would have these chores to do in our own homes. We weren't to grumble about it, as girls, we would just have to accept it.

Then one Monday afternoon as we came home from school on the fourteenth of July, a fuss and commotion was going on in the kitchen with pans of water being carried upstairs and Granny Ward told us we had to stay outside and play, she would call us in soon enough she said.

Presently we heard the wail and cry of a baby coming from Ma's bedroom and, down the street, we saw our new Pa wearily coming home from work. He was tired but not surprised to see us outside playing. We ran to greet him and told him about the fuss going on and that we weren't allowed inside the house. He quickened his step, and we all followed him up the stairs as he carefully opened their bedroom door.

Ma was sitting in bed in her nightdress with her hair tied simply away from her smiling face. She was holding a tiny bundle. A baby!

Pa stepped forwards towards her as she held the baby towards his outstretched arms.

"Your son," she said, proudly beaming at him as he gently took the bundle from her. "We have a boy."

Pa was speechless as he sat on the side of the bed gazing at his little boy, our new brother. He finally looked up at us and over at Ma, with the hugest smile on his face and tears of joy in his eyes.

"Joe," he said finally. We'll call him Joe."

We were allowed to kiss his little face just once each and then Granny Ward guided us from the room, leaving our parents with their precious son.

"Your Ma needs to rest now, girls. Come on I'll make you some tea."

Just then Grandpa Ward came in through the front door carrying a wooden crib that he had made. He was a carpenter and had been making this crib since he found out that he would yet again be a grandfather, this time to Joe's first child. It had rounded rails on the bottom so it would rock and a canopy at one end, which would cover baby Joe's little head. The wood was polished and shiny. Inside it was a quilted pad of thick material and a beautiful, knitted shawl that Granny Ward had made to cover our new baby. Eunice wanted to put her doll in it, but Granny wouldn't let her. She would tut under her breath and shake her head, feigning annoyance yet hiding a secret smile at everyone's excitement.

To say that we all loved our new baby brother would be underestimating the depth of affection we felt for little Joe. Ma fussed the most of course but even we three girls fretted if he sneezed or cried. Even when he was asleep, we worried over him, one of us would always be there by his side, holding his tiny hand as he slept in his crib.

We would tiptoe around the house when he was sleeping and fuss and play with him if he was awake. We would talk to him and show him our dolls and promise him that we would show him all our toys when he was bigger. Sometimes when he slept so soundly after a feed, Ma would softly blow on his face, his tiny nose would wrinkle up and his little lips would pucker into a kiss. That way she knew he was only sleeping and hadn't died. Looking back now, that was our greatest fear. None of us could bear it if Joe had been ill or God forbid, had died in his sleep. We were all totally obsessed with our new baby and none more so than Joe, our Pa.

He would rush home from work and, whether asleep or awake would lift Joe from his crib and rock his son in his arms so tenderly. Before he left the house in the early morning, he would give Joe one final kiss on his fuzzy little head before departing with his flat cap on his own head.

On Sundays when Joe was still small, Pa would carry him in his arms to Church and then back again. Then he would carry him to his parent's house or for a little walk in the fresh air over to the canal where we used to live to show his new baby son to all his friends. I'm sure that everyone in Failsworth had been shown this miracle - as if he were the only child that had ever been born; such was the love, devotion and pride we all shared for our little boy, Joe Ward.

He was baptized wearing a beautiful christening robe that Granny Ward had made. Her father, William Hulford had woven the silk many years before and she had kept a piece of it for this very reason. It had flowers and swirls embroidered in cream embroidery silk down the woven silk front panel, with lace on it that matched the lace we had on our dresses. It was a gown fit for a prince and we all wore our pretty princess dresses again to welcome him into our family and the family of the Church of God. Aunt Emily, Joe Taylor who was Joe's best man at their wedding and Allan Hollingworth-Hampshire from the post office at the corner of Wrigley Head and Oldham Road, stood next to our parents at the font as his God parents. Joe was as good as gold and peacefully slept in Ma's arms all the way through.

A celebration tea was held at Granny and Grandpa Wards house and because it was summertime, we ate sandwiches and cake at long tables outside in the sunshine. My whole family were all here together, The Humphreys, the Ellershaws and the Wards. Only Daddy and Minnie were missing but I had them close to my heart and their memories secure in my box.

Now it was late September, and the sun was still shining. We three were playing in the street with some other children, Billy Edwards and his younger sister Evelyn who lived next door to us, and little Alice Ashton from South View. Her ma and mine were good friends and Mrs Ashton was sitting in our kitchen having a cup of tea and a gossip with Ma.

Billy's Pa was a steam engine driver, and he was pretending to drive a train up and down the street collecting passengers. We all held onto the waist of the child in front of us, forming a chain as we climbed aboard Billy's train.

"Woohoo! All aboard!" he yelled. "Chhhhh chhhhhh, chhhhhh."

Billy shunted his train up the footpath, across to the other side of the road and back down the other side.

"Billy stop!" shouted Evelyn from the back of the train. "We're there. We're at Blackpool!"

The train came to a slow shunting stop. "Chhhhhhhhh," whistled Billy the driver, as the train let off its steam.

We all got off the make-believe train. Billy, Alice Ashton, and our Lizzie were having a race to the imagined sea at Blackpool to dip their toes in the make-believe sea. I was helping Eunice and Evelyn pretending to dig in the imaginary sand to build sandcastles.

We had no idea where Blackpool was as none of us had ever been, but that warm Saturday afternoon when all was well with our world, imagination was everything.

Chapter seven

Helping Ma

My dress sleeves were rolled up to the elbows and although I was taking the best care, my dress was wet all down the front. Lizzie held a tea cloth in her left hand and a plate in her right hand that I had just washed in the now almost cold water. I had rubbed it as best I could and placed it upside down on the wooden draining board.

"That's not clean Beatrice," she announced placing the plate back into the water for me to do again.

"You splashed me!" I cried back at her. "My dress is all wet now!"

"You need to do it again!" she stated with an assumed air of authority that she had adopted from Ma.

I scowled back at her and rubbed the plate again. "There!" I said annoyed at having her boss me about.

"That's better," she said.

"I've finished!" I snapped, untying the apron from around my waist, throwing it to the floor and marching out of the room.

I went to sit on the front doorstep that Ma had said needed to be swept and rubbed with the donkey stone. That should have been my next job, to donkey stone the step. This job was as boring as the other menial tasks we had been made to do and involved rubbing the sandstone doorstep with another piece of sandstone and a bucket of water so that the colour was even all over. This was apparently the mark of a good housewife and a measure of how well the wife kept her house. The job could wait for me! I wanted to just sit here in the early June sunshine and not do any boring housework.

Baby Joe was almost walking now, and Christmas had passed with great excitement at how well the child was making babbling sounds, strengthening his legs when bouncing while being held. Rolling about in his crib and turning over to reach for toys, only to instantly put them in his mouth.

Now my little brother Joe chatters all the time, saying "Bababababa" or "Mamamama" and everyone thinks that it's wonderful. He points at things and gets whatever he needs and picks things up for himself. He's crawling a little now and trying to pull himself up too. His favourite game is peek-a-boo. But it was mind-numbing. It was all so repetitive.

"Hello, grumpy!" said a voice behind me. "I thought I told you to stone the step."

I groaned.

Ma sat down beside me on the dirty step. "What's the matter?" She asked quietly. Ma had a way of knowing when I wasn't happy. I suppose mothers always know their children the best.

"I'm bored Ma. I'm bored of washing up dishes and sweeping the floor. I want to do something nice."

"Sometimes, my love, life is boring. Sometimes we must just live through the boring and wait for something nice to happen," she reasoned.

"Granny Ward said she'd show me how to play the piano, but she doesn't, ever. Whenever we go to her house, she fusses over Joe and there's never time for me. Even at Christmas, she said she would but then it was too late, we had to come home because Joe was tired. It's not fair!"

"Are you jealous Beatrice?"

"No Ma. I love Joe, really, I do! It's just that life is boring. I get to go to school and see my friends, but all I do here is clean dishes and help you and that's dreary."

"Well, you're a girl and you have to accept that this work has to be done," said Ma. "It's a fact of life and you'd better get used to it for when you grow up and have your own house, your husband will want it clean. But life can be nice too Beatrice. Don't you remember how nice Aunt Emily's wedding was a couple of months ago? You now have a new uncle Henry too. We had a lovely day at the Chapel, didn't we? Oh, and Emily looked beautiful in her white dress with that stunning wide brimmed hat, you liked her hat, I know you did."

"Yes, I did, she let me wear it when we went to her house after tea. It was so lovely." I hugged my knees with the memory of Aunt Emily's wedding hat. "Why didn't Aunt Emily go to the big Church like you did Ma?" I asked.

"Henry Roberts is a Methodist, my love, the Wesleyan Chapel is his Church, but it's all the same to God," she replied. "You will find many more nice things in life as I do. I have you and Lizzie and Eunice and now we have Joe. You all make me so happy. And, even nicer," she looked around to see if anyone else was listening, "we are going to have another baby," she disclosed with a little furtive grin. "I've told you first, so you and I share an exciting secret."

I tried to smile as I hugged her around her thickening waist and rested my head on her bosom. I stayed there for quite a long time. I didn't know what to say. A huge part of me was happy but I had an overwhelming sense of dread that my dreams of learning to play the piano or doing anything exciting, were drifting further away with the realisation of what a woman's lot in life was about. Just to have babies and to cook and clean.

"Come on," Ma encouraged, as she loosened my grip and struggled to get up off the front step. "You'll be seven soon. I promise we will do something exciting for your birthday."

"Humph!" I retorted. "Do I still have to do the step?"

She looked back at me with a silly wide-eyed smirk and tossed the donkey stone to me.

I scrubbed my anger away on that horrid step until it gleamed, that sunny day, and later that night, by the time Lizzie and Eunice also asked me why I was being moody, I was starting to feel better.

Ma had promised a nice birthday surprise and Eunice had told me that she had been singing with Aunt Emily again today. I was very happy for Eunice, as her voice was just so perfect. She sang like a little songbird, sweet and shrill. She sang perfectly in tune and with a great range, high and then low.

Lizzie on the other hand had spent her afternoon, like me, doing the cleaning for Ma. She had finished the pot washing and had to wipe down and dry the whole area as we had made such a mess fighting. She then had to sweep and then mop the whole floor. She had taken the rug outside and beaten it with a stick to get rid of all the dust and dirt. Then she had taken a cloth with some wax on and polished the table and the chairs and the pine dresser. We had also acquired from Granny Ward's house, a dark wooden cupboard that Ma had placed in the front room. That was lovingly polished too. Then Lizzie had taken another cloth and with soap and water, she had cleaned the inside of the windows, upstairs and down, polishing them with a piece of chamois leather.

I think Ma was more pleased with Lizzie than she was of me that day as, whilst she praised Lizzie, she barely said thank you to me, but I suppose I deserved it, I had been sulking.

Once again, our birthdays passed that year by taking a picnic to Boggart Hole Clough for my birthday. It wasn't as warm as it had been the year before and yet I still completely enjoyed my seventh birthday. Granny Ward had made some little buns for us to take with us and we had a big jug of ginger beer that Ma had found for a fair price on the Saturday market. We collected flowers and then had placed them in little posies flat in between two pieces of blotting paper. We then opened our big bible, placed the paper inside and closed the book. Ma said they would dry out and we could keep them forever.

Then in July, when the sky was the palest blue with fluffy clouds that looked like raw cotton, we walked over Ashton Road to Crime Lake for a joint birthday celebration for Lizzie's ninth and Joe's very first birthday, which of course was a great time for celebration, yet bringing bittersweet memories for all of us. Joe was almost walking for his first birthday and was growing stronger by the day. He was now fun to play with and we all enjoyed teaching him new things and showing him the little flowers in the grass or the big trees above our heads. He tried to copy some of the things we said too, which had the three of us rolling around in fits of giggles. He would watch us, bemused, and then laugh too throwing his arms in the air, squealing and kicking his chubby legs with excitement.

Later in the summer, for the first time ever on the 24th of August, we spent the day at Daisy nook for Eunice's fifth birthday. Nine weeks was between my birthday and Eunice's; with Joe's and Lizzie's in between. Summer was always so much fun and Ma showed us that life could indeed be fun and exciting and that there were always new experiences to be had and new places to visit.

On Friday 2nd October 1903 our newest little sister was born. We were unaware of the fuss this time as we were all at school and Aunt Emily was sent to meet us on our way home. She said we couldn't go back home until after tea and we followed her to her new house on Old Road where her husband had his cobblers' shop.

A huge pan of 'tata ash was bubbling away on her stove when we got there, and we devoured a dish full each with a huge chunk of bread that we mopped up the gravy with.

When we finally got home, Pa was stood in front of the fire holding his new-born baby daughter. He was yet again completely delighted by her safe arrival, and he decided that he would name her after his mother and our Ma.

She was to be called Sarah Alice. She was a tiny little thing and she captivated us all. Even Joe would pull himself up on the side of the crib to try to kiss her at every opportunity he got.

One Sunday a month later, Ma wrapped Sarah up warmly and allowed Pa to take her to show his friends as he had done with Joe. Lizzie and I went with him, leaving Ma, Eunice, and Joe inside where it was warmer by the fire. We walked down George

Street towards the canal close where we used to live.

The weather was cool and there was quite a strong breeze, which foretold of rain to come. Sarah was snuggly wrapped in her blanket with a little knitted hat on her head. Pa held her closely inside his jacket and his scarf was tied securely around his neck to keep out the draft. Lizzie and I wrapped our shawls around our heads and pulled them tight around our shoulders, crossing our arms in an attempt to keep out the cold.

"Brrrrr! I'm cold," said Lizzie. "Pa, can we go back please?"

"In a bit. I just wanted to see if Owd Bert was still here," he answered, referring to an old chap who plied his barge up and down the canal delivering felt from the mills in the Yorkshire hills.

We sheltered around the side of the lockkeeper's cottage until Owd Bert's barge safely entered the lock. As the barge rose in the water and was level with the towpath, Owd Bert climbed stiffly off to untie his rope. He looked up and caught sight of Pa with his special little bundle.

"Ayup Joe!" he called as Pa opened his coat to show the scruffy-looking old man his child.

"Eur fine lass o' thy own!" he said to Pa in his thick Yorkshire accent; then he nodded to Lizzie and me.

Breathing heavily, he peeped inside Pa's coat and took a long look at our little sister. He stepped back, nodded, and touched the front of his cap as he hobbled back onto his barge, clicking to his horse as he made his way out of the lock and onwards, back towards Yorkshire for another load of woollen felt.

That was the last time we saw Owd Bert. Apparently, about a fortnight later he had died. "Summat on 'is chest," reported another of the bargemen and the news had travelled back to Pa.

"I thought he didn't look well," Pa said when he found out. "That's another one gone!"

Joe was sat on Pa's knee banging two small blocks of painted wood together. "Ta," said Pa, taking one out of Joe's chubby fingers then giving it back to him, repeating the word "Ta!"

"Ta," repeated my little brother.

"Pa... Pa, listen to me sing," begged Eunice jumping up and down.

She cleared her throat "ahem!"

Clasping her hands in front of her, tilting her head up a little and posing towards the corner of the room, she started to sing; clear and sweet, a most beautiful little song that Aunt Emily had taught her.

We all clapped when she finished, and Sarah woke up crying with the noise we all made. Ma bustled over to pick her up to soothe her. The last few days Sarah had been a little unsettled, a little wheezy and her cries were more like the wail of a kitten. Ma nodded her head at Pa, signalling him to get up from the rocking chair so that she could feed Sarah although she didn't seem to be feeding well at all, she was weak and looked to be losing weight.

We were told to be good and to quietly go to bed. Pa helped us with Joe, and we put him in between Eunice and me. Somewhere in the night Joe had managed to turn around completely and had uncovered me. One of his chubby feet was across my chest, and he was almost pushing poor Eunice out of bed. His tousled hair, his long dark eyelashes that dusted his chubby cheeks and his cherry red lips that were puckered in a kiss, made me smile and a love for my little brother filled my very soul. I covered him and Eunice as best I could with the threadbare blanket and reached for my shawl to cover myself.

I lay in the early morning light listening to the stillness in the house. Life outside was beginning, and I could hear the tap-tap-tap of the knocker upper as his long stick knocked on the bedroom windows to wake the workers and rouse them from their beds.

Still in the early morning light, I tiptoed down the stairs to find Ma fast asleep in the rocking chair. I looked into the crib and leaned in to kiss my sleeping baby sister. My lips softly brushed the pale skin of her cheek. It was stone cold. Curious, I touched her with my finger. She didn't move, she didn't pucker her little blue lips or wrinkle her nose.

She wouldn't wake.

She was nine weeks old.

She wouldn't wake, ever again.

Chapter eight

Life goes on

We walked hand in hand in silence back down the path, away from the grave under the weeping willow tree where we had buried Sarah Alice with our sister Minnie.

None of us spoke, we just silently walked. Lizzie, Eunice, and I hand in hand, following behind our Ma, Pa and Granny and Grandpa Ward. Each one of us was stunned at what we had just watched: The laying to rest of the most innocent of babies, whose short life had barely begun; now lying with her sister who hadn't even reached the age of two years.

Joe had been left at home with Aunt Emily and she greeted us with a cup of tea and cakes as we arrived back. She tried to be cheerful.

"Joe's been fine," she said smiling as Ma rushed in, scooped up her little boy and buried her face in his neck, her hand cradling the back of his head as she sobbed and rocked Joe in her arms. His little legs wrapped around her waist, his arms around her neck and his head on her shoulder. He can't possibly have known what was happening or how we all felt that day, but I don't think any of us felt quite as wretched as Ma.

"Sit down love," whispered Pa, his voice was weak and croaky.

She sat down on the rocking chair still holding securely onto Joe. Eunice kneeled on the floor and placed her head on Ma's lap. Ma stroked her curls. Small solace, the four of us weighing against the pain of the two children she had lost.

Lizzie and I sat on the floor cross-legged nibbling on one of the buns that Aunt Emily had given us, while Pa sat at the table, his head in his hands.

I don't know how long we all sat there while the tea stewed in the pot but eventually Pa looked up and over to Aunt Emily. He nodded over to Joe, now fast asleep on Ma's knee.

"Alice," she whispered. "Alice, shall I brew another pot of tea? This one's gone cold."

Ma opened her eyes as if waking from a bad dream. She nodded. "Yes, please love. Here, take Joe from me. I'll do it. Time enough for crying, we must go on," she said firmly as she sat up. Joe's ruffled warmth had creased Ma's skirt and Aunt

Emily lifted him carefully from her arms. She placed him down gently on a blanket that Pa had folded on the floor in front of the fire next to me. He didn't stir as she tenderly placed a cushion under his little head.

"Didn't your Mam and Dad come in Joe?" she asked Pa.

"No, said they'd leave us be," he answered.

Aunt Emily fidgeted about. "I'll have to be off in a bit," she said, looking worried. "I'll have to get Henry's tea. He'll be wanting his tea when he finishes work. He'll be cross if I'm not there."

"That's alright love," answered Ma, sounding a little stronger. "You get home, I'll have to manage now; I have to go on I suppose." Such an air of acceptance and finality belied her shattered spirit.

"See you all later," Aunt Emily said quietly. "You know where I am if you need me." She nodded at Ma.

"I'll walk with you Emily," said Pa unexpectedly. "I need a pint."

Aunt Emily gave a little wave to us all and blew a kiss over her shoulder to Ma as she went through the door, wrapping her shawl around her head and shoulders against the December weather.

Pa stood up, laying his hand on Ma's arm as she stepped towards him with a worried look on her face. "Won't be too long," he stated. "I'll walk

91

Emily home down Old Road first, but I'll only have one."

After they left, Ma gave a large sigh as if she had lost the strength to be a mother or a wife. She looked quite adrift as if she didn't know what to do with the kettle she had in her hand. Lizzie scrambled to her feet and took the kettle from her.

"I'll do it Ma. Sit down."

Ma sat back down on the rocking chair and watched as Lizzie filled the kettle with fresh water from the jug and placed it on the trivet above the fire. Then she took out the teapot with the stewed cold tea in it and emptied it into the waste pail by the back door. Next, she reached for the tea caddy and put a carefully measured teaspoon of loose tea into the teapot and placed it on the table. We all watched the fire in silence while we waited for the kettle to boil.

Eunice had come to sit on the rug next to me and I helped her untie her boots. They had first been Lizzie's boots and then mine. Now they were Eunice's boots. We all had clogs for school and that was fine during the warm weather, but when it was cold or raining the clogs rubbed our feet and did nothing to keep our cold toes warm. Aunt Emily's new husband was a bootmaker and she said she'd ask him if he had any spare leather to make some boots for us, but nothing had come of it and so we wore our clogs and waited for boots.

Pa worked hard but he didn't bring in much money. Not enough to buy us all boots anyway. Ma couldn't go back to the mill either because of the babies, Joe and then Sarah Alice.

I don't suppose anyone dares ask her if she might now. It wasn't a question for today.

"Ma, I'm hungry," whined Eunice.

"Oh goodness, silly me!" answered Ma. "I think we have some bacon in the meat cupboard and there's some bread. I'll fix us a buttie and then you girls can tidy up and get to bed. You all have school again in the morning and I've done no washing today, Monday and I've done no washing!" She was flustered and distracted. "Oh dear!" she added as she got up and went to fetch the meat and bread.

Joe stirred and sat up. I reached over and pulled him towards me and started to pile up some wooden blocks into a tower. He swung his arm and knocked them all down. He was happier knocking them down than stacking them up as I had intended him to do. Every time I piled more than four up, he would knock them down, cheering as they fell.

"Ma the kettle is boiling, and I can't lift it," said Lizzie.

"Oh dear," replied Ma again. "Oh dear," she flustered about to pour the boiling water into the teapot to brew the tea.

After we had finally eaten our supper, Pa came home later than expected.

Ma scanned his face and he smiled at her. His smile could melt ice.

"I only had a couple," he said by way of an explanation to her unspoken question. "I called into the Church Inn on my way back from Emily's, and Joseph Taylor was there. I've not seen him since Joe's christening. He said how sorry he was and sends his condolences."

"Oh, that's nice," said ma as she turned away. She handed him a plate with a large chunk of bread, bacon and a piece of cheese on it.

"Supper," she stated. "Hope it's not cold."

Lizzie and I exchanged glances and kept quiet.

School the day after wasn't as bad as I thought it might be. Most of the girls were gentle with us and sympathetic. Most of them had also lost brothers and sisters as babies, some had lost parents too and death was something that touched us all. Many diseases and countless reasons for dying surrounded each one of us, as I was growing up. Typhus fever, factory accidents, childbirth, tuberculosis, and pneumonia were only a few of the reasons that people were taken away from us all before their time, and certainly long before we were ever ready to lose them.

I thought often about my daddy. Ma had said it was tuberculosis. I still missed him. Minnie died from a disease in her tummy called an ulcerated bowel and now poor little Sarah Alice had died from tuberculosis too. It wasn't until many years later when I had asked Ma why people had been taken from me, that she explained all this to me, but those days at school only showed me that I was not alone and that we had all lost so much in our young lives.

I didn't have to try very hard at school; I enjoyed most of the lessons and was very good at reading, writing and arithmetic. I could easily multiply big numbers and I was always top of the class. Ma would save the paper that was wrapped around the meat or cheese that she bought so that I could practice my handwriting every day and I had a chalk board too.

My teacher Miss Jones, a tall lanky woman would always pick me out as an example to the other children for spelling.

"Beatrice! Spell friend," she instructed.

I stood up with my hands clasped behind my back. "F r i e n d."

"Spell continuity."

I did.

"Sit down, very good. Billy, spell build!" she ordered.

Billy stood up. "B... i... l... d," he stammered, red-faced.

He was made to stand in the corner facing the wall until the end of the lesson. Poor Billy, his ma had a baby last week. Both the baby and his mother had died, but a week was considered long enough to get over it.

I understood that year, the year that I was seven years old, that people are born, and people die, there is no scheme or reason behind it, and we can do nothing except watch and live on. No matter how much we might want or need them to live, they don't. I also learned that sometimes other people don't really care or feel the pain that you do inside.

A consequence to all this is the realisation that certain people live on, and some are given more time alive than others. I learned that time could appear to pass rather slowly, childhood gradually moulding me into a kind and sensitive, accepting yet optimistic person. Now I realised that the days of my childhood passed far too quickly and the days that I would have liked to have lingered in, were the shortest.

Christmas came and went again that year and very soon the winter fogs and rain, cold winds and snow subsided. Warm weather returned and June was hot and muggy. The sun tried to shine but the smoke from the factory chimneys and the coal fires made it hard for us to see the sun.

"Will it be Boggart Hole Clough again for your birthday?" asked Ma as she popped her head around our bedroom door.

"I don't know," I responded listlessly. "It's too warm to go anywhere." I lay on my bed without stockings, just in my underclothes. The window was wide open but that only seemed to let more warm smoggy air in rather than cool me down. Lizzie had a paper fan and lay on her bed gently wafting it over her face. Eunice and Joe were outside in the yard playing with a bucket of water, a large pan and some tin cups. She was showing Joe how the little cup could fill the big cup and back again, we could hear them laughing and splashing which was the only relief from the oppressive heat.

In the end, we didn't go anywhere. Ma was sick. She had been sick for the last few weeks, every morning.

Granny Ward made a party tea at her house for my eighth birthday instead and finally, she took me inside the front room and let me sit down on her piano stool next to her. She showed me where middle 'C' was, how to spread my fingers so that they covered eight keys for an octave so that my little finger also played a higher note 'C'. Then, how to keep the same finger spacing for an octave in the key of D, then E and so on.

The sound was incredible. I was in raptures. I had made that sound; me, with my own long slim fingers. I was entranced and two full hours passed with her showing me how to start with my right thumb then each of my fingers and how to bend my thumb under my little finger so that my thumb played the sixth note and my first two fingers the seventh and eighth of the octave to play a scale. She showed me how to make little tunes and how to remember which finger played which beautiful perfect note.

I think I can now say that my eighth birthday was one of my most memorable. I threw my arms around her in grateful thanks when it was time to go home, and she promised she would let me play again another day.

Also, memorable that year was the birth of yet another baby girl to Ma and Pa. She was born on the 12th of December 1904, again while we were at school, but this time Grandma Humphreys had looked after Joe and had made a pea and ham soup so that there would be food on the table for us when we came home.

This time Pa decided that our new sister would be called Sarah Annie. Again, she was a perfect little doll of a child and was very well behaved. She seemed stronger than Sarah Alice had been, she slept well and fed well, and she grew, and she thrived.

It was with the birth of Sarah Annie that I realised just how fast time did pass. My earliest memories were of the little cottage between the canal and the railtrack, with all its dirt and deprivation that was unseen and acceptable by familiarity to a three-year-old child. I remembered my warm and strong Daddy, and how time stood still when he went away. Ever since then, the time has flown by. I had a sister, Minnie who we loved very much but she died and then we had a brother, Joe and he is growing up fast and strong. He will be three years old this summer. Then Sarah Alice was born but then she also died before we even had the chance to get to know her.

Now Sarah Annie is growing well and yet we all seem to be on heightened alert. Ma and Pa seem tense as if they are holding their breaths, waiting. Time this year seems to have slowed down and the spring seems a long time coming. Easter was very wet and there is a lot of illness in Failsworth and farther afield in other towns too. The mundaneness of life is ever-present and if we are not in school, we are helping Ma to clean the house. Ma has a big pin that she fastens to the hem of her skirts to lift it off the ground so that it doesn't get sullied with the mud and dirt as she does her cleaning.

Tedium, while we wait for summer to come, while the earth waits to warm up for the plants to grow, the trees hold back their leafing and the sun hides behind large clouds of billowing smoke from the factories.

Some days it is difficult to breathe.

Chapter nine

Steam kettles and

bad water

Eunice said that her throat hurt because the air was so thick some days. She and I stood watching Ma filling a strange-looking kettle with water. It had a funny long spout, and it made a lot of steam when it was heated up on the fire.

"What's that for? enquired Eunice.

"It's a steam kettle," Ma answered.

"See, I told you so," I boasted. "A steam kettle, that's what I said it was."

"Yes, but why, what's it for?" she asked again.

"It's to produce steam to help Sarah Annie and you breathe. You said your throat hurt and the baby has been struggling to breathe too, she's had a cough for a few days," answered Ma again: yet still only giving a partially full explanation to her two inquisitive daughters.

"Sit on the chair and place your head over this bowl," Ma told Eunice. When she did, Ma covered her head over with a cloth that also covered the bowl.

"It smells horrid what is it?" She asked, lifting her head from the steaming bowl again, allowing a waft of steam to escape.

"Some peppermint from grandpa's garden. Breath up your nose Eunice and don't talk. Get the steam into your chest."

Ma then covered Sarah's crib with a sheet and attached a long tube to the steam kettle so that she could fill the crib with steam for the baby to breathe in.

"There, that should help," she muttered to herself. "Beatrice, can you please peel some potatoes while I watch this."

I went to the cupboard and picked up the bag of potatoes, I took out four of them and an onion. I pulled all the little sprouts off the potatoes and the green shoots that were sprouting from the top of the onion. I then managed to remove the papery skin off the onion and chopped it up into pieces with a sharp knife. Ma had taught us to be careful and always chop away from our fingers. Then I scrubbed the potatoes and rinsed them in the clean water bucket. It was hard, but I cut them into pieces and put them in the big pan with the onion and poured over some water from the jug until the potatoes were covered, just as she had shown me. I stood back proudly surveying my work.

"Now what Ma?" I asked. "What else do I do?"

"There's a beef knuckle bone wrapped in paper in the meat cupboard. Rinse the sawdust off it and put that in the pan too."

I did as she said, the bone was big and slimy. "Ewww! I can't lift the pan Ma," I said, wiping my bloody and wet hands down the front of my apron. "Ewww, yucky!"

"I will do it. Thank you, Beatrice," she said to me with a proud smile. She took the sheet away from the crib and placed the steam kettle on the hearth to cool down.

Eunice sat up from the steamy bowl of water, her eyes were watering, and her face was wet.

"My throat feels better now Ma,"

The baby slept on. She hadn't woken for a good few hours, and while this was nice, it wasn't right and there were little dark shadows under her eyes. She had been on solid food for a few weeks now and seemed to be enjoying new tastes, she liked potato mash or milk paps or oats that Ma fed her. Ma was wary and quite vigilant, looking for any stomach problems that Minnie had experienced in case Sarah Annie might be ill, as Minnie had been. She had been just as attentive when Joe was at that stage but now, he's nearly three and he has no problems eating. He's quite a little rogue and we all love his spirit and energy. He's a happy child and very bonny. He loves looking at picture books with us and drawing patterns with my precious crayons that Grandma Humphreys had found for sale on the Tommyfield market in Oldham.

Ma watches over her precious baby, always listening to her breathing too in case she became weak like Sarah Alice was before she died.

Sarah Annie seems fine, and Granny Ward tells her not to worry. She gurgles happily to us as we play and talk to her. She kicks her little legs as she watches our faces and reaches for the toys that we show her; she puts everything we give her into her mouth, and we are very careful not to give her anything too small. But these last few days she has been weaker and less eager to wake up to eat. Ma was uneasy and although Pa tells her not to worry too, they both do.

But then that's what mothers do I suppose. They sense things that no one else does. They worry and care when no one else notices that something is troubling. She knows when we were happy or sad or feeling ill. She understands our moods before we can recognize the thoughts in our own hearts. A mother's love is endless, non-negotiable, and yet so fragile and brittle. She cries when we are hurt and tries her very best to mend our troubles before considering herself. If we ever push away her love, she will weep in solitude but come out smiling for us again whenever we need her love.

Mothers instinctively know when something isn't right. Ma's gut feeling was now troubled. I could see it in her eyes, in fact we could all feel it.

After she had put the pan that I had prepared, onto the fire to cook she tried to wake Sarah Annie for her feed. She carefully lifted her out of the crib, but she was floppy and cried when Ma woke her up. She held her to her breast and at first, she suckled for a few minutes, then fell back asleep as if she were exhausted.

There was a knock on the door and a friendly voice. "Cooeeee! It's only me Alice!" Mrs Ashton's head appeared around the door. "How is she?" she enquired as she sat herself down at the table and looked at the sleeping child in Ma's arms.

Ma looked up at her, in despair. "She won't feed for long Margaret, and she's hard to wake. I tried the steam kettle and it just seemed to make her sleepier," she replied shaking her head, she lowered her voice and leaned towards Mrs Ashton. "I think it might be pneumonia. I spoke to Mary next door. She had two babies who died from it before the two she has now. The younger two are both all right thank goodness, but she said hers wouldn't feed and were asleep most of the time. Then they got as they couldn't breathe… and then they died," Ma said, her eyes filling with tears as she looked down at the fragile life she held in her hands, as if powerless to stop the impending rollercoaster of loss.

"It could be I suppose," answered Mrs Ashton, forgetting that I was there. "You've got the others though, that's a blessing. Have you tried the linseed poultice?"

"No. What's that?" Ma asked, trying to wake the baby to feed once more.

"It's, a sort of mixture made with very hot gruel and linseed, then you must put it onto her chest between two layers of cloth. It's supposed to draw the badness out. I'll get some for you in the morning."

The conversation went on, but I didn't want to hear that this baby sister might not be strong enough to make it. I didn't want to hear that we might wake up one day and her skin be cold like the last sister I had lost. I didn't want to hear the truth, that Sarah Annie would be placed in the ground with her sisters.

I wanted to stop time again so that this baby would not die too. I placed my hands over my ears and tried to ignore what was being said by reading the same page of my book that I had already read, trying to stop the sound of my heart from banging in my ears.

A week later, however, that is just exactly what happened. Not quite three weeks before my ninth birthday, this delicate life was snuffed out and we would once again watch a small white coffin be lowered into the ground beneath the branches of the weeping willow tree in Failsworth Cemetery.

Sarah Annie, a third sister now lay in the cold dark earth with Minnie and Sarah Alice; forever sleeping.

Happiness had been sucked out of the house again. Our birthdays passed but with no delight whatsoever. Granny Ward showed me some more tunes on the piano, but her lessons didn't go into my brain. There was no joy in it for any of us.

We were all bewildered. Lost in the confusion. Trying to understand the loss and to figure out what could be learned from our miserable life.

Babies die too is what I had learned. Babies and Daddies and yet I had nothing to place in my box to remember Sarah Alice and Sarah Annie. Just my brief memories of lives ended before they began. There was a numbness I couldn't explain.

An empty sound in my ears. An ache in my heart.

If I thought for a moment that death and disease would leave my family and me alone now after all that had happened, I was sadly mistaken.

Not very long after we had lost Sarah Annie, Granny Ward started to be ill in September when we went back to school. Grandpa Ward said he thought she had eaten some bad meat and had been sick for a couple of weeks.

"I thought she were on the mend," he said with a worried look on his face as he came into our house late one afternoon a couple of weeks later. "She couldn't keep even water down but seemed she felt a bit better yesterday. Now she's a throwin' up all over again. Can you come and see her Alice please?" he asked Ma.

"Of course, I will," answered Ma. "How many days is this, Henry?"

"About ten I think now," he wrung his cap in his hands. "I'm worried sick, she's startin' wi' a fever and said she's awful pains in her stomach."

Ma took a quick look at Pa and the four of us sat around the table eating our thin soup in silence.

"I'll just wash up these dishes when the children have finished tea and I'll come up home with you," she answered. "Joe, do you think you should come up too?" She looked over the table to Pa, it was a statement rather than a question and she had a worried frown on her face. "Lizzie, be a good girl now and look after the others please."

Don't miss the last train home

"It's alright Ma, we will do the dishes. You and Pa make sure Granny is alright," Lizzie said. I looked up at my big sister, full of admiration for her at rising to the challenge. Eunice and I nodded our heads in agreement. I took the spoon from Joe and scooped the last drops of soup from his dish for him.

"Open!" I instructed. He opened his mouth for the soup.

"Ahhhh!" he said, wiping his mouth with the back of his hand. Copying the way Pa did the same when he finished his soup.

Grandpa ruffled the top of Joe's head with his hand and the three of them left us to go and see to Granny.

"Let's play a game when we've washed the pots," I said. "How about hide and seek?"

Once the dishes were done and put away, I took Joe's hand, and it was our turn to hide first. Lizzie counted to one hundred while we went upstairs. Joe and I wriggled under our bed to hide, and Eunice crouched beside the chest of drawers in Ma's room. Lizzie found us straight away of course, there was no fooling her, and the game began again with me starting to count.

"One, two, three…" I peeped through my fingers to see Eunice disappear out into the back yard and I continued to count.

"Coming ready or not," I shouted opening my eyes to see little Joe sat in the corner of the room, crouched down as tiny as he could, with his small hands over his eyes, his knees tucked up to his chin.

"You're supposed to hide Joe." I chuckled.

"You can't see me!" he giggled. Silly thing! He thought that because he couldn't see me, I couldn't see him. I joined in his game and pretended to look for him.

"Joe," I sang, pretending to look for him everywhere else. "Are you under the table?... No! Behind the rocking chair?... No! Where are you, Joe?"

He sat very still hiding his face behind his hands, giggling to himself. I soon found Lizzie and Eunice. I put my finger to my lips and pointed at Joe and we all faked looking for him until he jumped out at us.

"Boo!"

I don't suppose I was worried about granny. She was poorly but I didn't quite know what that meant exactly. There had been weddings and more cousins born over the last three years since Ma and Pa married and Joe and the babies were born. We had lots of Humphrey's cousins, aunts, and uncles still. We had lost two sisters, but we had gained an uncle John when Pa's sister Nancy got married last year: and Uncle William, another of Pa's brothers had a little boy called Harry. They already had a little girl called Annie who was a year older than Joe and the two avoided each other as best they could, which amused us all. Uncle William and Aunt Sarah brought the children to our house a lot and it was nice to have baby cousins in the house. It helped us to play with them and for Ma to be able to heal her heart from losing her own babies. It was nice to be part of a big family although Pa's oldest brother Elijah had taken his wife and little girl Phoebe to America six years ago, long before Pa came into our family. Pa's sister Alice and Uncle Arthur also had a little girl called May who was a year younger than me, and she was nice to play with too. Sometimes we would all play hopscotch outside on the pavement.

The words that I had heard long ago when we buried my handsome Daddy; 'The Lord gives and he takes away," made much more sense to me now.

Ma looked more worried when she came home later that evening. Pa had gone off to the pub. She was pleased that we had tidied up and had kept Joe occupied. It would soon be time for bed, but Ma went upstairs and packed a few things in a large bag before coming back downstairs to us.

"Where are you going to Ma?" asked Lizzie, our spokesperson.

"Lizzie, you're eleven now and I expect you to be a very big girl and look after the others for a few days," she said seriously. "Pa will do what he can to help but he'll have to go to work, and you'll have to look after him too. I am going to look after Granny, she's quite poorly and Grandpa can't manage on his own. Uncle Tom and Aunty Margaret will help me. I will come home every day to see if you are alright, but I won't come in in case I make you ill too. I will look through the window every afternoon and if you need anything, Lizzie, you must go to fetch Aunt Emily immediately."

"Oh, Ma!" Lizzie exclaimed. "Will granny die?"

Ma sighed and put her arms protectively around the three of us, little Joe sat on the floor at her feet and hugged her knees. "We think it's typhoid, she has a fever and very bad pains in her tummy. Now Lizzie, you must boil the water before you drink it, always leave it in the big jug over there." She nodded to the kitchen dresser. "Oh, girls, I love you all so much!" She placed a kiss on each of our foreheads as we looked up at her. Then she bent to kiss Joe too.

"Be good!" she instructed as she went back out of the door, out into the October night, to care for Granny Ward.

Chapter ten

Beer and no piano

The only tangible thing I had to remind me of granny Ward was the one singular birthday card that she had given to Ma the first time we met her. On the front was a fuzzy picture of a farmhouse surrounded by trees. On the dark blue sky were printed the words;

> MANY HAPPY RETURNS
> *Tis only a simple postcard,*
> *But it carries my message true,*
> *A bright and Glorious Birthday,*
> *Is the wish I send to you.*

and on the reverse, she had written

> *Best wishes*
> *From Mrs Ward.*

The card had been stood on the dresser but had slipped down behind a large plate, where it remained hidden from view for four years, until I found it again while Ma was away looking after Granny. I took the card upstairs and placed it in my box. I sighed and wiped the tear from my cheek with the back of my hand as I knelt on the hard floorboards next to the bed. I now had three cards in my box.

I remembered the very first time we had gone to her house and met her and Grandpa Ward. How warm we had felt, how happy and welcome. Embraced into their home and family. The sweetest of little cottages; their vegetable garden, full of cabbages and potatoes and the row of flowers that Granny loved to grow; the smell of that first Christmas meal; the sound of her playing the piano; all memories that will stay with me forever.

She had given this card to Ma for her birthday that year, the year before we had lost Minnie but gained a whole new family. Now she was gone too, and I would never see her round face again or see her smile when she was pleased that I had remembered what she taught me to play.

She would teach me no more. I sobbed quietly to myself and slowly closed the lid on my box.

So…daddies, babies and now grandmothers die too!

"Why, Ma? Why?" I had asked, sobbing when we were told the news.

"Because we are all human I suppose love," answered Ma with an insight that only an adult can comprehend. "There are diseases and illnesses that people can't get better from. Some people live longer than other people: that's all I know. What is important is how we live Beatrice, that we are good people, kind and helpful to everyone. We must keep our faith and believe that life goes on. We must love each other while we are all still here together and pray each night that God protects us."

"But he doesn't," I argued back, gulping down sobs. "He didn't protect Minnie or Daddy or the babies… or Granny!"

"Hush child," she murmured into my hair, as she rocked me on her knee on the rocking chair, curled up like a baby myself. "I have no answers Beatrice, I hurt too."

We rocked for a while longer. Me, a nine-year-old child curled up as small as possible on her knee like a baby; her, my comfort, strength, and warmth; together in our grief and pain.

After Granny Ward's funeral, Pa went to the pub instead of coming home with us. When eventually he did appear, he was rather the worse for wear.

We children had gone upstairs to get ready for bed and Joe was fast asleep already when we heard Pa downstairs. He was swaying and banging into the door as he came staggering in.

"I'll drink if I want to!" he shouted. This was his answer to whatever Ma had said about the state he was in.

Lizzie stopped undressing and crept towards the door to listen. Never had we heard him raise his voice to Ma before. I had been sat on the edge of our bed brushing my hair ready to tie it into a plait for sleeping and Eunice was already under the blanket next to Joe. She had been singing a lullaby to him.

We all held our breaths and waited to hear anything more, but it was quiet.

"It's my guess Ma has told him to be quiet," Lizzie whispered.

We breathed more easily then and carried on getting ready for bed. None of us heard our parents coming upstairs later. Perhaps we fell asleep so that we wouldn't hear. Perhaps we wanted to shut out any more hurt.

But more hurt came.

Only a month after we had lost Granny Ward, Pa's older sister Mary Ann, also died. Uncle Ernest came to tell us, and Grandpa Ward said he would place her in the grave with her mother in Failsworth cemetery.

Don't miss the last train home

I don't think for a moment that any family had ever felt so low at that point. Pa sat for days with his head in his hands crying: Crying for his Ma and his sister and his two lost babies. None of us knew how to console him and I had never seen a man cry before.

We were so low that Christmas was a non-event in our house that year. It came and went as if we couldn't bear to smile or feel any joy.

Pa often drank. He would not always come straight home from work on Friday payday and would always be late for supper.

As he came into the house in various states of drunkenness, Ma quietly took the rest of his pay from his pocket and tucked it under her apron. She understood his pain, she understood how much he must hurt but she also understood that the rest of us needed food and that the rent needed to be paid.

Early in the New Year I also found myself in trouble and at first, I couldn't understand why. One afternoon as I came home from school, I saw Ma sat in the rocking chair with a letter in her hand.

"Beatrice!" she said angrily. "What is the meaning of this?" her face infuriated, her eyes wide. I was immediately frightened and wanted to run away.

I stood in front of her, head bowed with my hands clasped in front of me trying to understand the fury in her voice.

Ma was never angry with us; we knew we were all good children.

Ma usually understood and gently explained if we were out of order. She was never cross with us, but today, something in her voice told me to be cautious. My precious schoolbooks, tied together with string, slipped slowly from my grasp, and clattered to the floor.

"Why have you been doing Lizzie's homework for her?" she demanded.

"She... she can't do it herself Ma and she... she asks me to help her," I explained innocently. "She can't do her sums as well as I can, and she... she was in trouble for not doing her homework."

"Is this the first time?" she asked, still using her stern and cross voice.

"No Ma," I admitted. "I... I always help her."

He shoulders dropped a little and her voice softened a little.

"But it is you who is in trouble. This letter is from school, and they want me to go in to explain."

"Lizzie has struggled with her homework since Joe was born Ma. I tried to show her how to work out the answers, but in the end, it was easier to do it for her." I knew I was in trouble, but I was so

118

confused. Why does helping someone always get me in trouble?

"It should be Lizzie who should be told off!" I looked up at Ma, tears welling behind my eyelids. "Lizzie, who couldn't do her sums, not me. I could do the sums easily and she's two years older than me."

"Yes, I'm extremely proud that you are very clever Beatrice love, but you are the one in trouble and you shouldn't have done her work for her," Ma's anger was subsiding now, as she understood the whole situation.

"I'm sorry Ma," I said quietly. I hung my head, looking up at her under my lashes. I saw a small smile creep onto her face as she pondered the situation. She pursed her lips and slowly folded the letter as if she had solved a huge mystery.

"Where is Lizzie?" she asked.

"She's hanging about at the end of the street with Eunice and Elsie Haslam… and a boy called Alex," I disclosed; but knew then that I had said enough.

"I told you all to come home together. Always!" she shouted, cross again.

"Sorry, Ma," I repeated. Guilty of nothing except by the implication of knowledge; I knew Alex rather liked our Lizzie and he followed her home from school every day. Today, she decided that she would talk to him but because I walked

119

faster and couldn't be bothered with boys, I got home first.

"Go and get them both please." Ma said, getting up and placing the letter on the table. "I need to speak to Lizzie."

I made my escape, leaving my schoolbooks where they had fallen. Eunice and Elsie had carried on walking and were home, gossiping like little old ladies outside our house, pointing and giggling at Lizzie and Alex further down the street. I skipped off and down to the end of the street where Lizzie was leaning on a low yard wall on the corner of Wrigley Head and Alex was sheepishly kicking stones about in the gutter.

"Lizzie!" I shouted as I approached them. "Ma said you're to go home straight away. She knows about the homework!"

They both looked at me and Alex blushed. He hastily said "bye," and ran off in the opposite direction, ducking down the alley way past South View and into Ellesmere Street.

"Now look what you've done!" Exclaimed Lizzie. She stormed off past me to go home to face her own music. Likely she wouldn't speak to me for a day or two but at least the truth was out.

I followed her back slowly and held Eunice back before she followed Lizzie into the house. We stood at the front door while Lizzie faced Ma and tried to explain her way out of the mess and apologise for getting me in trouble with the teachers at school.

We could hear Ma shouting and it was hard to stop ourselves laughing.

"Lizzie, you will be twelve soon and will be leaving school to go to work. If you get a job in the mill, you will be expected to work hard and be able to keep up with everyone else. You won't be able to get anyone else to do that work for you. You got Beatrice in trouble and that is not nice at all!" Ma lectured Lizzie for over ten minutes, while Eunice, Elsie and I stifled giggles on the doorstep.

"And I won't have you courting boys on the way home from school!" she added loudly as she sent Lizzie up to our bedroom in disgrace.

Ma was still angry after supper when Pa came home, drunk again, as was becoming the usual state that he came home.

"We don't have the money for drink, Joe!" Ma would say every time he came home. But it fell on his deaf ears. He didn't want to know; he didn't want to hear. He was hurting.

I think we all understood how he was hurting. The rest of us hurt too, but everyone had to carry on. We had to go to school and Ma had to look after her family.

Pa was hurting and had to continue working but he drank to try to hurt less he said. He was a platelayer on the railway. It was a hard manual job with long hours and not much pay. He was out in all weathers, laying and maintaining the rail track. His work had to be done in-between the trains coming and going and if the rail wasn't secured in place properly, there could be a disaster. If the gang of men he worked with misread the train timetable, they could get hurt or killed. Perhaps this too was why he drank.

He thought it gave him the courage to carry on. Ma put on a brave face; she had to, for the rest of us.

Her friend Mrs Ashton understood. That year she sent Ma a lovely birthday card. It was embroidered silk mounted on card with blue forget-me-nots, pink flowers and green leaves, and the words A Bright Birthday was also embroidered on it in blue. Ma thought it was very sweet and it brought a tear to her eye when she read the back where her friend Mrs Ashton had written,

> *A token from a friend to a friend. Wishing you many happy returns of the day.*

I coveted that birthday card, and I was caught looking at it every day until Ma finally allowed me to take it upstairs to place in my box. It seemed the only happy card that I had, and I realised that I smiled when I looked at it rather than feeling sad as I did for the other cards in my box. I smiled because I knew it made Ma happy and sometimes, I took it out to let her look at it again whenever she looked sad. She always smiled at me, and we shared that warmth.

Lizzie had to start work that summer. She was twelve years old, and she had to go to the Ivy Mill and sign up for work. The first day, she came home quite excited at the world of work and what she had seen and been allowed to do. They had tried her at many jobs. First, she went into the carding room where the cotton was teased and brushed straight before it was spun. Then they showed her the spinning looms where hundreds of strands of carded cotton were spun into thread. The damp air of the Pennines was considered favourable to spinning the finest of cotton thread. And finally, she was shown the weaving rooms where the cotton thread was woven into the smoothest of cotton fabric.

"Cotton fabric from Manchester's mills is considered the best on earth and shipped all over the world," she boasted to us as if we didn't already know.

So, she started work in the carding shed and came home exhausted at the end of every long day with cotton fluff in her hair. Happy that she could give Ma some money now to help with food for us all and more confident in herself.

In mid-August, we were yet again at another wedding. This time it was Pa's youngest sister Annie who married John Schofield, a local coal miner. It was a lovely wedding and Annie looked so grown up.

I told her how pretty she looked in her dress.

"Happiness makes you pretty, Beatrice. That, and the love of a good man," she answered smiling up at her new husband as he tenderly gazed down at her.

To an innocent ten-year-old little girl, growing up in a rather austere world where I had already lost so much and had been hurt so much, it sounded to me like the answer was there in her words…

Love…Love would make me happy.

I looked forward to the day when I would be swept off my feet like a princess, madly and deeply in love with a handsome man. He would carry me away to a paradise I knew nothing of yet but would only dream about until I would be grown up too.

So that day I learned that love would make everything right. I was ten and so eager to grow up. Love would take away the hurt and the poverty. The hardships of life, the long hard hours of toil, the pain of losing people in our life, would all magically disappear when I would eventually find love.

So, I wait, and I dream.

While I wait and dream the hard life goes on.

Chapter eleven

Temperance comes home.

Pa came home from the pub many, many times in an appalling state of drunkenness. It made us both sad and angry that a lovely, kind and hard-working man could succumb to the evils of drink.

There were posters everywhere calling out the immoralities of alcohol and I was now seeing it in my own home. The posters showed how 'drink steals children's food.' They showed men beating their wives because of drink; posters saying that 'drinking leads to neglect of duty, moral degradation and crime'. Posters and public meetings were held begging men to give up the 'demon drink'. Frightening posters for children to see when they knew they were unable to stop or even help their own parents. We begged Pa to stop drinking but he always said he would and that he didn't drink much.

One Saturday morning when I went with Ma to the market at the end of Wrigley Head, I found a young girl handing out posters for the Juvenile Temperance movement and I excitedly took one from her. Lizzie and Eunice agreed with me that we should join. The next meeting was the following Thursday and we said we would ask Ma if we could go.

I was very worried to see Pa stoop so low. Although he never raised a hand to Ma, and I don't think he ever would hurt her, things were not as they once were in our house. They would argue about Pa drinking, they would quarrel about money or lack of it, and each would blame the other for the deaths of our two babies and Minnie. Arguments always made worse depending upon the amount of drink that Pa had consumed.

We knew he hurt and yet we could not ease the wounds that he carried in his heart. He did not know how to rid himself of the unhappiness inside, the pain and agony of loss that he felt. He said that it had all happened so fast. One day he fell in love and before he knew it, he was married with a son and us three girls as his own.

Completely happy he was, he often said. Then it all went wrong, his babies died and then his mother and sister. He couldn't cope with that loss and so he drank. He knew he shouldn't, but it was all he had to help him.

The problem was that it only served to make it all worse.

Many, many times his friend Joseph Taylor brought him staggering home. Pa's arm slung over Joseph's shoulder, with Joseph half-carrying this torn and dishevelled man back to the bosom of his family. Ma would help to undress him and get him upstairs to bed and always said thank you to Joseph for bringing him home. She pleaded with them both not to let Pa get into this state but almost every week he would.

When sober, Pa worked hard and long hours, but it was as if his light had gone out and he no longer cared. Little Joe was almost five and Ma had managed to get Pa to promise that we would have a nice party for him with a few of his school pals. A little picnic was planned for them on the Sunday afternoon of the 14th of July.

Late one Friday at the end of June however, Pa came home, again in a stupor and over the shoulder of Joseph Taylor. He half-carried him and half dragged poor Pa into the house, and they staggered in, falling in a laughing heap on the floor in front of Ma. She stood with her hands on her hips, visibly upset and yet again furious that he was in such a state.

"You're all wet Joe!" she exclaimed. Get up off the floor you stupid man!"

"He got wet Alice." drooled Joseph, trying very hard to be serious, but failing. The pair of them rolled about in fits of giggles, cackling and uttering stupidities.

"Shhhh!" giggled Pa. "You'll wake the children."

"Too late!' shouted Ma, kicking out with her foot at the pair of them on the floor. Her foot caught the back of Pa, and he raised his arm to punch back but she stepped niftily out of the way.

Ma stepped over them, she went to the front door, softly closed it, and put the bolt across, then she came towards the stairs where Lizzie, Joe, Eunice and I were stood in our nightshirts, cowering together like frightened rabbits watching the sorry events unfold.

"Upstairs!" she ordered, ushering us up the stairs and back into our room. "They can stay there all night for all I care!" she slammed the door to her bedroom, and all was quiet until morning.

We were all cross with Pa. He wasn't a drunkard, a wastrel. No! he was such a lovely, wonderful man and a great father to us all. This wasn't just about him; we had all lost the same people as he had. Ma was grieving for her babies too, but she had to carry on. She had to hide her pain and couldn't give in.

Ma had to survive. We all needed to survive. Pa was taking all the attention when we all needed love and care too.

He was ill in bed for the next couple of weeks with a very bad cold and fever. He felt very sorry for himself.

Then it turned to pneumonia the doctor said.

Pneumonia! The very word struck fear into our hearts, horror and dread set in.

That's when we stopped being cross and started to worry. We fetched him soup and bread, we brought him herb tea to drink. Ma set up the steam kettle in their room to help him breathe. We took turns to sit with him, holding his hand and talking to him so that he knew we were there with him. Eunice sang to him, and Joe would climb in bed beside him when Ma wasn't looking and fall asleep by his side.

The night before Joe's 5th birthday, Pa was fast asleep. His breathing was heavy and laboured as if he were climbing a steep hill. Ma mopped the beads of perspiration from his forehead. She begged him not to leave her, over and over she begged and cried. He held his weak hand up to her face and touched her wet cheek with the back of his fingers.

"Shhh." he whispered. "It's alright love."

She held his hand to her and kissed the back of his hand while holding it to her face. The night was still, and the room was warm and dark with a deep foreboding: quiet and yet menacing. The only sound was the steam kettle hissing out its vapour.

Eunice kept Joe in our room, oblivious and unaware of how sick our Pa was. Lizzie and I stood in the doorway to their room, barefoot once again, watching another good man die. He opened his eyes and gazed at Ma, their eyes locking together, heavy with secret unspoken words; he moved his head to look towards us in the doorway where we stood hand in hand. He smiled at us one last time as his loving heart stopped beating.

He lies forever now with Minnie and the babies, under the weeping willow tree.

Ma had no tears left.

The Lord takes away and he also gives.

Just ten days later new life came again to the cottage at 57 Wickentree Lane. Ma helped Aunt Annie when her time came and rather than be present at a death, Ma delivered life. Aunt Annie and Uncle John had a little boy. She gently handed the new-born Jack to Grandpa Ward and in his grief, he wept tears of happiness.

We all did.

Life surely goes on and times were most certainly hard. Life without Pa was enormously difficult. He had shown us all such love and kindness in the brief time that we knew him, and Ma refused to give in to emotion. She forgave him for his drinking, saying simply that love conquers, and we should always understand that.

I wasn't too sure. How can love hurt so much and how can I ever trust or love for myself when the pain of loss is so great?

Lizzie wasn't so sure either when we talked but she had always been more optimistic than me. She was the romantic one, believing that one day her prince would come. I believed that too but there was a deep worry in my heart that there would always be death or pain. Whatever the Lord could give, he would surely take away.

I had turned eleven just before Pa had died and Lizzie was now thirteen. She was now a woman of the world, out working in the mill and busy making new friends. Alex still followed her around and then there was Eddy Doyle. He had quite a crush on her, and the two lads would try to outshine each other for her attention. Flirty madam she was! She let them follow her but paid them little care or kindness.

Grandpa Ward often came to our house for tea. He would always bring vegetables from his garden.

"I don't know if I can dig the garden over this year," he said. "I get so tired these days since Sarah went. My heart ain't in it." He held a bunch of greens and some carrots that he'd freshly dug up. He stood in the doorway as if he didn't know whether to come in or not.

"Come in Henry. Sit down, you make the place untidy," joked Ma. "I'm sure the girls, Joe and I can come up and help you dig. Wouldn't we?" She asked. We all nodded in agreement and so the following weekends we spent quite a lot of time up at Grandpas house, digging in the garden and harvesting the vegetables he had planted earlier in the year.

Muck was plentiful with all the carters' horses going past, and whenever there was a fresh pile of muck on the road, Grandpa diligently went out with his bucket and gathered it up. He piled it up in the bottom corner of his garden and let it rot down.

"Beautiful muck," he said every time he placed more on his growing pile.

"Now we have to fork it into the earth and let it work its magic over the winter. Joe, you get that barrow and Lizzie help him to fill it up. Then you can dump it here so the others can dig it in," he instructed.

Ma pinned up her heavy skirts with her big pin, to keep them out of the dirt. She was eager to learn and get involved. I think it healed her heart to do something so satisfying as digging.

We all got on with the jobs Grandpa ordered and soon the ground looked dark and fertile, moist and full of goodness ready for the next years planting. A couple of little robins followed us about the garden, feasting on the worms and insects that we turned over. One of them was very cheeky and sat on the edge of the barrow, waiting for worms. After a few weeks of digging, Joe had managed to get the little robin to take a worm from his outstretched hand, so trusting was he.

Sprouts and parsnips were harvested after the first frosts and by Christmas, we had decided that we should all have a meal together like we used to. Our loved ones might have departed, but their love could still be felt when we were all together.

At Easter the next year, Grandpa said we had a very special job to do in the plot where we had put all the muck. He proudly brought out a bag of wrinkled potatoes, all with little white sprouts on them.

"Eugh!" we all said when he opened the bag.

Grandpa laughed and showed us how to take off all but one sprout and how to place it in the ground, sprout up and cover it over with the soft fertile earth.

Ma would diligently walk between the rows, hoeing out weeds and watering the ground until eventually the potato haulms grew large, and flowers started to appear.

"When the flowers die back, we can dig 'em up. Lovely fresh new potatoes, now't like 'em wi' butter on," said Grandpa, licking his lips and chuckling to himself. "There's a flower and vegetable show on at the Methodist Church, Alice, would you like to enter it?"

Ma thought for a moment and looked from Grandpa to Joe's eager face. "Yes, why not?" We've all worked hard enough, perhaps we might win," she smiled.

That Saturday in early July, we all helped to dig up ten of the biggest potato plants, leaving the rest to grow on. We were all amazed to see creamy white potatoes appear from the dark succulent earth, tippling out as Ma dug in her fork, pulling it back towards her. We helped to pick out all the potatoes, brushing off the soil with our hands and gently placing them in Grandpas basket. Next, we cleaned them with water from the pump and he showed us how the skins should be clean and perfect. The flawless ones went into one pile, and the ones with marks on or greening went in the basket for use in the kitchen.

We chose twelve of the largest potatoes and decided which were the best matched to sit together for the show. Eventually, we had three plates with four potatoes on each, ready to be carried over to the chapel on Oldham Road for the show that afternoon.

There was much hustle and bustle in the chapel room with people milling around, placing their exhibits on the two rows of long trestle tables. One was for flowers and arrangements and the other for vegetables. There was another table at the end for cakes and craftwork.

Joe led the way with Ma, Lizzie and me, each carrying a plate with our carefully picked potatoes on. Grandpa and Eunice followed behind, eyeing up the other exhibits. We walked down between the tables until we found a gap with a small card that read 'Mrs Ward' on the white tablecloth that covered the table.

"Here it is Ma!" shouted Joe and we carefully placed our competition entries down.

After about half an hour everyone was instructed to leave the room so that the judges could assess the entries. We were told to come back at three-thirty for the prize giving.

Excitement was now building, and just after half-past three the head judge, an officious looking round-bellied man in a stiff white collar and smart suit, banged his gavel on the table in the corner and a hush descended the room.

Flower entries were judged first, and prizes were given out, to great rounds of applause. Then the cakes and crafts were next.

Joe was so excited he could hardly contain himself. We're going to win; we're going to win!" he whispered to himself over and over.

So sure, were we all that we were going to win, that we were not in the least bit surprised when the round-bellied man said, "The first prize for three plates of new potatoes goes to Mrs Alice Ann Ward!"

With a huge cheer from her supporting team, Ma stepped up to the front of the chapel to collect her prize of a shiny new copper kettle.

Chapter twelve

The iron handle

"It makes a lovely cuppa, Alice," Grandpa said, once we were home and Ma had made a pot of tea with the new kettle.

"I hardly want to get it dirty on the fire," Ma answered handing a plate of bread and cheese to him. "Wasn't it fun?"

"Will you enter again next year, Ma?" Eunice asked.

"That's a lot more digging!" Grandpa joked." It's all down to the beautiful muck!"

We all laughed together at that, and we all forgot about being sad, just for a while.

A month later I had been told that I had to go down to the mill gates to sign up for some work. I didn't want to do it. I didn't want to work, I wanted to stay at school. I enjoyed school and although many of the other girls in my class were twelve too, they were eager to start work, but I wasn't. Many of them had to work to help to bring in money for their families and I suppose that is why I agreed to it, not that I had any choice really. Since Pa had died, we had struggled a lot and Ma had taken money from the parish so we could be fed. Now I was twelve and of working age, and so I had to work - like it or lump it!

Lizzie had been working full time for over twelve months and she said it was alright. She worked very long hours and she always came home tired. Ma had also gone back to the mill part-time when Joe started school and we have a lovely photo of him in his jacket and white-collar. It stands next to the one we have of Minnie on the dresser.

So now it was up to me to grow up and get to work to help bring money into the house. I gathered my shawl around my shoulders and followed Lizzie across Wrigley Head, our clogs clattering on the cobbles as we were joined by many other workers wearily trudging towards the noise and grind of the mill at six thirty in the morning.

It was a warm sultry sort of day, with the sun still low in the morning sky, hidden behind the haze and dark muggy clouds as it always seemed to be. It was a rare day indeed for the sun to shine and for us to see any glimpse of blue sky. I remembered my Daddy and just one happy day, many years ago when he lifted me high and carried me on his shoulders when we walked down through Moston Brook. He said if I was to reach up high enough, I would be able to touch the sky. He said if I could grab him a little piece of the blue sky, he would put it in his pocket and keep it safe forever. I remember that I reached up with my little hands, arms outstretched, but somehow the blue was just too high and far away, and I've never since been held on anyone's shoulders as big and strong as my Daddy's.

Lizzie said her goodbyes at the mill gate, and I joined the queue of girls my age to be allocated a place.

I had always thought the mills to be big buildings from the outside, but once within I was astounded to see just how big the floors were. I was taken to the weaving shed. The machinery stretched from side to side, from grotty window to grotty window, great noisy clattering looms with huge cones of cotton and hundreds of strands of cotton thread being fed constantly down to the hundreds of weaving beds. Men and women bent over the looms, their hands working so fast I couldn't see what they were doing, keeping the yarns and the shuttles flying. The smell of oil and grease attacked my senses and the sight of the powerful machinery working, filled me with fear; great shuttles travelling backwards and forwards, clattering and whirring, the noise was frightening.

I didn't like it; I wasn't happy at all.

I told Ma I didn't like it but she just looked blankly at me and so I had no choice but to go back day after day and finally Friday arrived. The foreman counted out some coins into my outstretched palm. That was the best part of the whole week and Ma said I would be able to go down to Wrigley Head market on Saturday and choose something nice for myself, as it was my first week's wage. The rest of my pay after that would have to help to buy food.

Lizzie and I got up early on Saturday morning and she excitedly showed me her favourite stalls. Some of them had ribbons and buttons, and one had some pretty printed cotton fabric. I chose a light blue one that reminded me of the sky that day long ago. Printed on it were some tiny pink flowers, with green leaves and yellow swirls also printed on it. I politely asked for three yards and paid the lady my money. I felt as if I had suddenly grown up that week. I decided that I would make a skirt and Lizzie helped me to find some blue ribbon to match it, for me to wear in my hair.

I bought Eunice and Joe a quarter of boiled sweets to share and a small trinket pot in the shape of a swan for Ma. The swan's body was green and covered in pretty, pink flowers, a ring of blue forget me nots edged the top and on the chest of the swan was a lilac rose. The graceful white neck and head of the swan rose and bent over so that its beak rested on its chest. Ma placed it on her nightstand. She said couldn't be cross with me spending money on her when I bought her something so pretty, she had said.

The weeks went on and the noise became normal to me, so the fear subsided a little. Every Friday I got my pay, and I gave it to Ma. Lizzie always sulked a little when tipping up, but I didn't want for much myself. Pretty ribbons or trinkets didn't fill a family's bellies.

I'd only been working a month when, one Tuesday in September, Aunt Emily was in our house, crying and shaking in Ma's arms.

"He's gone," she sobbed. "He's gone, my Henry. He's gone."

Ma held her and Lizzie and I hurried over to comfort her.

We learned through her sobs that Uncle Henry had been poorly but that morning at work, had collapsed over his bootmakers last whilst hammering nails into the sole of the boots he was making. His head had fallen forwards and his friend and co-worker, William Hall had thought he was fooling around.

"His heart gave in," cried Aunt Emily. "He's gone. How will I manage when the baby comes? Oh!" she wept. "He so wanted a son." I could see that she was almost collapsing so Ma guided Aunt Emily to the rocking chair where she sobbed and sobbed, and the rest of us said nothing in disbelief.

Just before Christmas, Aunt Emily's son arrived. She called him Harry and she carried him each Sunday to the grave where she had buried her beloved husband just three months before.

Ma helped Aunt Emily as best she could, repaying her for all she had done for us in our first grief, and a month later, we were present as our cousin Harry was christened at the Wesleyan Methodist Chapel where Aunt Emily had married Henry Roberts just six years before. It was a strange day, full of love and happiness but so very sad that another child would have to grow up without his father as we girls all did, as Joe did, and now Cousin Harry did.

Life went on as life does. Lizzie and I went to work, and we helped Grandpa as much as we could in his garden. The following year, Ma won another copper kettle for growing her potatoes. It was rather a standing joke in the family that Alice Ann had two copper kettles, one for weekdays and one for use on Sunday.

We grew rather fond of Cousin Harry, we played with him often and would take him for walks down through Moston Brook, over the humpback canal bridge, under the railway bridge, through the trees and along the river. He was a grand little chap, and he grew strong. Aunt Emily had inherited Uncle Henry's boot making business and shop on Old Road and had decided that it was too much for her and so she sold it to William Hall.

She decided that she wanted to go back to Trefonen near Oswestry where she had been born, to give Harry a country childhood. She found employment with a family that her mother, our Grandma Humphreys knew. She was to be housekeeper to a gentleman by the name of Thomas Jones whose wife had died and his six children, aged from twelve to one year old, needed looking after. By the time cousin Harry was three, Aunt Emily had married Thomas Jones and she wrote often to tell us how the family were and how Cousin Harry was growing up so fast.

Our life changed a little too at that time. Eunice now joined Lizzie and me in the mill, but only part-time as she was still in school too. Lizzie and I now worked in the carding room where the cotton was combed and teased into strands for spinning.

Eunice was in the weaving shed, she had to crawl under the machinery to clean up the fluffs of cotton so that it didn't get into the woven fabric.

That year also we moved to number 5 South View. It was a small cottage, tucked away in a cobbled courtyard of four cottages, just behind Ellesmere Street and off Wrigley Head. It was where Ma's friends, Mr and Mrs Ashton had once lived, and they had moved onto Oldham Road. We now lived next door to the Melling's at number 7. The other side lived Mr & Mrs Borwick in number 3, and Mr Sidebottom lived alone in number 1.

Eunice and I shared a bedroom, with just a small window in the corner overlooking the yard behind the houses on Wrigley Head. Lizzie moved into Ma's room and Joe had a little box room all to himself in the attic, he had to climb up some rickety steps to get there but he was happy. There was no back yard, and it was much smaller than number 42, Wrigley Head but the rent was less and that made it alright.

The box under my bed had gained a few more cards, postcards from the seaside from Mrs Ashton and Lily, her little girl and several from other friends and family. Birthday cards too; I kept them all even if they weren't mine, the others would let me keep them in my precious yet increasingly tatty box. I would sit on my bed and look at them all whenever I had a quiet hour, they brought back lovely memories both happy and sad, and I looked forwards to one day perhaps visiting the seaside myself.

There were allotments down George Street behind the Wrigley Head Mill, not far from the canal and the Albert Street lock where we used to live, and Ma took one, spending many happy days digging, planting and harvesting vegetables and even some fruit from her little plot. She often said she would like some chickens for eggs, but Grandpa said the fencing wasn't good enough to keep foxes out and so the idea was shelved.

One spring afternoon, while Ma was busy at the allotment, we were allowed to wander off on our own to explore. Ma had wanted us to follow Joe and his pals so that he wouldn't get into any mischief. Lizzie was sixteen, and out of view of our Ma, she would meet up with Alex and secretly hold his hand when she thought no one was looking. I knew, but I'd never dare tell Ma. She also sometimes met up with Eddy Doyle and being the tease she was, would tell Alex that Eddy had asked to hold her hand too.

Joe and a few of the other lads he knew were kicking a ball about and scuffling about in the dirt, pushing and shoving each other about as only eight-year-old boys do.

Eunice and I followed the boys up along Wrigley Head and then left, down under the railway bridge and towards Wrigley Head bridge that crossed the canal. From there you could walk over Moston Brook to Moston. Today the boys took the cobbled steps on the left, that led round and down to the towpath, and we followed them; down through the cluster of trees that made me feel like I was entering a dark spooky grotto before it opened onto the light of the canal towpath again. It was a cool day, dry but with a cool breeze and it rather chilled the air.

Lizzie and Alex followed behind, secretly holding hands but pretending not to, and occasionally I heard her giggle at something he had said, and she would lean suggestively towards him. Once on the towpath Lizzie and Alex turned right and went to stand under the bridge, rather too close together for my liking.

He was trying to kiss her, and I was shocked. It was broad daylight!

The boys and Joe turned left and walked, or rather ran and pushed and scuffled with each other, along the towpath and back towards the lock at Alfred Street.

Eunice and I had to run to keep up with them and they wouldn't slow down despite our shouts. Lizzie and Alex followed, but at a distance that was growing wider and wider. I looked back to watch her and then forwards to watch Joe. I didn't know what to do for the best.

"She's grown up Beatrice, stop worrying," stated Eunice. She could tell I was getting anxious. "Ma said to watch Joe."

We hurried then to catch up with the boys and if I didn't know better, I think they were trying to outrun us.

We finally caught up with them at the lock and two barges were waiting to go in, with one already in the lock. The sluices were open, and the water was forcing its way through the gates to empty the lock to lower the water level so that the barge could carry on towards Manchester. A young boy stood with a horse while they waited; although I didn't think he needed to as the poor horse looked so tired, with its head down, not interested in the grass the young boy was offering it.

Joe and the others had crossed our humpback bridge and had climbed down the other side where the forbidden overflow weir was. We always called it our secret waterfall, never daring to climb down ourselves, but the boys had taken off their clogs and were splashing about in the water. Eunice and I stood on the top of the bridge both watching them and looking at the torrents of water surging through the lock gates. From the top of the bridge, it was a powerful sight to watch the turbulence below us.

147

Suddenly there was a shout, and someone yelled "Joe!"

Eunice screamed as she saw what was happening before I did. She screamed again, a loud piercing scream. I turned just in time to see Joe, feet in the air; slip and fall over the edge of the little waterfall and with a huge splash, he landed in the canal.

He went under the water straight away and that was when I screamed too.

"Joe, Joe!" I shrieked. "He can't swim!"

We ran over the bridge and down to the weir where the other boys were frantically trying to reach him with their arms outstretched, a couple of them lying down in the water of the weir, fishing around in the canal for my brother.

I lifted my skirts to try to get to him but of course, I could get no closer than they all were.

"Joe!" I shrieked.

Eunice was crying.

Joe's head bobbed up then, above the water. He spit out a fountain of water and took a huge gasp as he disappeared once again, his arms flailing.

"Joe!" I screamed again in panic.

Lizzie and Alex heard the commotion and came running towards us. They climbed down the opposite side of the bridge and Joe splashed and thrashed his arms over towards Lizzie. Slowly the lock gates began to open, forcing the water to swirl around menacingly.

Alex grabbed the well-worn iron handle that was fastened to the bridge and held on tightly; his other arm was around Lizzie's waist, and she clung onto Alex, her other arm outstretched to Joe in the water who was like a drowning young puppy, paddling and splashing towards her.

"Swim Joe!" Lizzie screeched. "Swim to me!"

Joe splashed, went under, splashed some more, but little by little he got closer to Lizzie on the other side, just as the barge emerged from the lock and glided under the bridge.

She leaned as far over to him as she possibly could and eventually, he reached her. Their hands met briefly as he slipped under again and Lizzie screamed once more.

Just then Joe lurched himself out of the water in one last effort to find her hand again and this time she didn't let go.

Eunice, me and the other boys had run back over the bridge to Lizzie and Alex, just in time to see Joe's face, wide-eyed and full of panic and fear as he grabbed hold of Lizzie's hand.

Alex couldn't let go of the bridge handle and Lizzie didn't have the strength to pull Joe out. I kneeled at Lizzie's feet and grabbed out to try to help Joe. I grabbed his shirt with one hand and the back of his pants with the other, and together we hauled Joe with one almighty heave onto the towpath at the side of the canal steps where he lay coughing, spluttering and panting at our feet like a landed fish.

Chapter thirteen

Rabbits

Eunice was visibly shaking; she fell to her knees and hugged the soaking wet Joe. Lizzie and I stared at each other and then down at the wet heap on the side of the canal.

"Is he alright?" I demanded, kneeling next to Eunice, and putting a protective arm around her shaking shoulders.

Joe coughed and spluttered and tried to sit up.

"Are you alright, Joe?" we all asked together.

"My goodness!" I exclaimed in relief. "You could have drowned, what on earth will Ma say?"

"I'm alright, stop fussing!" he answered waving us away with his hand.

Joe was more embarrassed in front of his friends, who were hanging about on the towpath now, all three of them looking very uncomfortable.

"He fell, it weren't me!" said one of them.

"No! It were 'im!" said another. "He pushed 'im."

Fingers were being pointed at each other, each one squabbling and laying the blame onto the others. Typical of boys I thought.

"Get up Joe," ordered Lizzie. "We'd better get you home and dry. I hope Ma's not in yet." She added with concern on her face.

We all climbed up the steps carefully guiding Joe by the hand, although he didn't really need three concerned sisters fussing him. He was able still to walk and talk, he protested!

They say they feel all right with bravado just to show off to their friends, but we wouldn't let go of him however much he complained.

We trouped back along George Street and across Wrigley Head, back towards home. By the time we got there, he was shivering. Much to our relief, Ma wasn't in and so Joe was able to get dry clothes on and before long he was warm again and laughing about the whole episode.

Ma came in about an hour later and would have been none the wiser had Joe not opened his big mouth, much to our disbelief as we had promised each other that we wouldn't tell Ma otherwise we would all be in trouble. Especially Lizzie, who had been courting and holding hands with Alex in broad daylight, when she had been told not to.

"I learned to swim Ma," he confessed before she had even taken off her shawl. "I fell in the canal and Lizzie saved me."

He recounted the entire story to answer Ma's many questions. When he had finished Ma shut her eyes and breathed a long sigh down her nose. She pursed her lips and looked at each one of us in turn with her eyebrows raised, as we stood with our heads and shoulders hunched, looking up at her, each of us expecting a scolding.

After a long pause, she calmly said. "Well done girls, thank you. I think you had all better not go down that way again. It's too dangerous to play near water. It's extremely busy with the barges and the horses and I'd rather you were all safe."

None of us answered.

We all loved walking down by the canal; it was full of interesting things. We were fascinated by the hard work of the canal people and the constant comings and goings of the barges, noisy, smelly and dirty. The world of industry that we had always known, the smoke and dirty rain in winter, thick yellowy smog that we had to cover our mouths with our shawls in order to breathe.

Yet the countryside in summer was beautiful. It was so pretty, and just over the other side of the two bridges that led to Moston Brook. It was our secret magical world full of bees and butterflies, birds and memories.

Lizzie started to protest, but I quickly nudged her and shot her a look. I knew what was in her mind.

"Grandpa knows a man who has rabbits and if you promise to not wander off Joe, especially with that rabble of friends you seem to be attracted to, I think I might let you have a couple. Would you like that?" Ma asked.

His pale blue eyes lit up and he promised her; we all did, that he wouldn't stray and most definitely would never go down to the canal, ever, ever again.

I wasn't too sure that the promise would stick, especially for Lizzie but for the moment we had managed to placate Ma and that was no bad thing.

I realized later that evening when I went upstairs, that she would have found out about Joe's escapades anyway because boys just don't seem to understand how to hide the evidence. I reached the top step and stood, in stockinged feet, on a pile of smelly canal-wet clothes that Joe had left in a soggy heap on the landing outside our bedroom door!

"Boys!" I exclaimed loudly, "How would they ever dry, left in a heap?" Then I smiled with relief that he had been saved, for I was mortally afraid that it could have been so very much worse. I gathered up the waterlogged heap and dripped my way down the stairs with them, throwing them outside into the yard.

The next Saturday grandpa arrived with two fluffy grey chinchilla rabbits and of course, we were all very excited to get to know them.

"Don't fuss them," Grandpa said. "Let them get used to you. They'll want cabbage and carrots to eat, and grass. I'll fetch some hay later. I've made a box for them to live in, but I'll make a run, so they don't get lost."

"What are their names, Grandpa? asked Eunice, fascinated by the little fluffy animals.

"Well, I suppose we'll have to find names for them." he answered, which set us all debating what names we might like best.

"The little grey one is the colour of dust, perhaps Dusty is a good name," suggested Ma. "And this one is darker with a white nose, what would you call him Joe?"

"Willow," Joe stated as if he had thought of nothing else and the name had come from deep within him. "The girl one is definitely called Willow."

"That's all agreed then. Willow and Dusty, welcome to South View." Grandpa said. "Is the kettle on Alice? I feel like a cup of tea from one of your two kettles."

He chuckled to himself at his joke and followed Ma inside.

I watched them go through the door leaving us with the rabbits, and I wished more than anything that Pa could be here to see them. We were so happy when Pa was alive. He was a lovely man and I loved him deeply, perhaps as much as I had loved my own Daddy. He was kind and happy before the babies died and grandma died, and he couldn't stand the pain of that. If they had lived, he would not have turned to drink. I knew he wouldn't, he was not like that at all. It didn't seem fair that we had to go on without him and try to enjoy things now that we were deprived of him. I knew he would have enjoyed seeing the rabbits and I felt so sad for Joe that his Pa was gone.

There was a low whistle from around the corner of the cottages and Lizzie peeped around to see who it was. She turned to me with a finger on her lips and slid away out of sight.

I could only guess what she was up to.

After tea, and after Dusty and Willow had been given a carrot each and 'put to bed' in a nest of warm hay. Joe stood in front of the fire and said, "Listen, Ma, listen to this that I made up."

"Rabbits, fluffy rabbits,
I like to watch you leap.
I like your twitchy noses,
Calm and fast asleep.
Long-eared, fluffy rabbits,
I like to feed you hay,

Don't miss the last train home

I'm happy now you've come,
To live with me today."

"Oh Joe, that's lovely," Ma answered with a smile, and we all agreed.

Over the next few weeks, the rabbits took up all Joe's attention and time. He sketched pictures of them and made-up little rhymes all the time. One little poem he even made a tune for and sang it day and night.

Now I can't get that tune out of my head, he sings it repeatedly. I caught Eunice singing it as she fed them both some hay one morning.

"Please can you sing a different tune, Eunice," I complained, and we both laughed.

The following summer, after a whole year of having rabbits, Joe's poems were getting rather good. He was such a dreamy child; deep in thought most of the time with a cheeky grin, light brown hair and pale blue eyes. He could charm the butterflies to land on his hand; he was such a gentle naïve boy.

Eunice too was very pretty, her hair she wore in long ringlets down her back and when she was younger, she would wear a large bow atop her head. Her face was round and full with a pert little nose. She was graceful and loved to dance and sing, her crystal-clear voice ringing out on a starry night when she would go out to see to Joe's rabbits and to say goodnight to them.

Ma had these two photographs taken and of course, I secreted them away into my box that I kept hidden under my bed. I treasure them both as the one with Eunice on also has Ma on it.

Lizzie and I are not so pretty as Eunice is and I don't have any photos yet of me that I like, as photography is very expensive. A photographer came to school some years ago and took a photograph of Lizzie in costume from a play she was in. I have that in my box too now.

We grew up as happy children and knew we were loved both by Ma and each other, of course. Joe and Eunice get along best together, and Lizzie and I are best of friends. Joe and Lizzie do fight sometimes, not fists, as Ma wouldn't allow that; but they do fratch.

I smile now about it, but I remember one time, a couple of years after Joe got his rabbits: Lizzie had been out, and everyone had thought that she was with Alex. Ma had agreed that she was old enough to go out 'a courting' now that she was seventeen and had been working for over 5 years. Many boys wanted to walk out with her, but Alex was the most persistent.

This one day it had been raining quite hard as it sometimes does in September. It was still summertime; quite bright but with a chill to the air and dampness in the mornings that reminded me that summer was almost gone. The rain had cooled the air, even though the sun sometimes popped out in-between the thick clouds of our Failsworth blue sky. The rabbits had been sheltering in their hutch, peeping out with their noses, sniffing the air, perhaps to check if the rain might have stopped. There were more than two rabbits now of course and I suppose this is how we all learned how baby rabbits were made. Willow and Dusty had been separated shortly after the first batch of baby rabbits had been born and Joe found homes for all of them.

Then he would put them together whenever he wanted to breed some more. Now, Willow and Dusty had eight babies that were about five weeks old, and we now had three hutches in our garden.

We were inside and I was halfway through reading 'A maid of the silver sea', a new book that I had found on the Tommyfield market in Oldham. Joe was writing yet another poem, looking up into the distance pensively until he came up with just the right word to note down in his poem. Eunice had just finished knitting a blanket that had taken her over a year, she was stitching all the loose ends into it, and all was calm. Ma had been at Mrs Ashton's house all afternoon and there was quietness and peace in our little modest home.

Lizzie was out gallivanting; I thought she was with Alex until there was a knock on our door and Alex popped his head around it,

"I'm looking for Lizzie," he said.

"She's not here," replied Joe without looking up from his writing. "She's out with another boy. I don't know his name."

There was a look on Alex's face that I couldn't describe. Surprise, hurt, anger. He quickly turned, and we heard the door slam behind him. Eunice and I looked at each other and Eunice blushed with embarrassment.

"Joe!" she exclaimed. "I told you not to say anything!" Obviously, there was more to this that I was being involved in. The tangled web that Lizzie was spinning was starting to come unravelled. I closed my book and asked Eunice what she knew.

"Where is Lizzie, Eunice?" I quizzed.

"I don't know," she stammered, then, turning to Joe she said again, "you said you wouldn't say anything! Now I'm in trouble!" She threw down her needles and her knitted blanket and stormed upstairs.

"Joe?" I queried, "What's going on? Who is Lizzie with?" I could see he wasn't listening.

"*Smooth, the boat glided....... smoothly, the boat glides,*" he pondered the words to his poem out loud and ignored me.

"Joe!" I shouted, demanding he snap out of his dream state and answer me. "Where is Lizzie?" I asked again.

"I don't know. She said she was out with a boy and not to tell anyone," he said looking innocently at me.

"But you did!" I exclaimed, "She's obviously not with Alex, is she?" I shook my head in disbelief.

Just then Lizzie strolled in and helped herself to a glass of water from the pitcher in the back kitchen. She sat down and didn't say a word, and so of course, neither did we. I picked up my book again and waited for Ma to come back.

Later that evening, after supper, Lizzie went upstairs, Ma and I washed the dishes while Eunice and Joe went outside to give the rabbits some carrots and to put them all to bed.

Then there was a cry and such a commotion from the front courtyard.

Shouts from Joe of "Come here!"

"I've got one!" shouted Eunice.

"Get Dusty, there he is!"

"Quick he's escaped!"

They're all out now! Help!"

Ma and I dried our hands and rushed outside to see Eunice and Joe running here and there with a baby rabbit under each arm, frantically trying to round the others up and to chase them away from the alley that led to Ellesmere Street and back towards the hutches by the wall.

Dusty and Willow were furthest away, and Ma and I exchanged sniggers as we knew quite well with what they two were up to that in a few weeks we would have yet more baby bunnies.

Joe eventually managed to get the young rabbits back into their run and Ma and I cornered Dusty and Willow just before they escaped up Wrigley Head.

I chanced a look up to the bedroom window, where I saw Lizzie watching the hullabaloo with a snide grin on her face.

Chapter fourteen

JJ and cigarettes

It had taken over half an hour for us to get them all safely back in the correct cages and to make sure there was no damage done. Joe and Eunice checked the cages and the runs for holes or any means of escape in the dimming evening light of late September. They were both frantic and upset. Ma was trying to stay unruffled and in control of the situation, cuddling each rabbit to check they were each all right.

I went upstairs once the rabbits were settled.

"What on earth did you let the rabbits out for?" I demanded. "It was you, wasn't it?"

Lizzie lay on her bed calmly reading her book, ignoring my questions. Her feet were crossed at the ankle, a satisfied grin on her face.

"Lizzie!" I reached out crossly to take the book from her in order to understand why she was so nasty to our brother by letting his rabbits out deliberately when everyone else thought they had escaped by accident. I knew it had been her.

She snatched her book away from my grasp; she carefully closed it and placed it on the bed next to her.

"Joe told Alex I was with another boy, and he was cross with me," she stated as she sat up and untied her hair from the bun she had carefully twisted on top of her head. Her brown hair tumbled around her shoulders, and she looked innocently up at me.

"But you were," I responded angrily. "Alex called here looking for you. He was very upset."

She smiled slowly, a satisfied twinkle in her eyes. "I knew he loved me. Beatrice. He said he didn't love me, and he wouldn't ever marry me. I was quite upset with him. I wasn't with another boy, I just wanted to know if he would be jealous if he thought I was."

I shook my head and frowned at her in bewilderment. I was either too trusting or didn't yet understand the complexities of courtship.

"You still shouldn't have let the rabbits out, Lizzie. That was very bad. I think you should say sorry to Joe and to Eunice. She's very attached to them you know, she's crying," I said as I left her bedroom to go into my own to prepare for bed myself.

"And…" I added sternly. "If Ma knew it was you who let them out, she'd be most cross."

"He has a friend Beatrice," she shouted after me. "A lad called John. He's noticed you a few times. I told him we could walk out together if you like."

I closed the door quietly so that she thought I hadn't heard. I had seen Alex's friend and thought he was a very nice-looking boy. There was something about him that made me feel shy and a little giddy. I was only just turned fifteen three months ago, and I couldn't understand what these feelings meant. My cheeks flushed as I thought about what she had said and quickly undressed and jumped into bed, the freshness of the sheets felt cool against my warm cheeks.

Over the next few weeks, I managed to avoid Lizzie and Alex and, by deliberate default, Alex's friend John James Hankinson. Lizzie told me he lived on Ashton Road West and his friends all called him JJ for short. He was named after his father, a coal miner. Not that I wanted to know of course, and I snubbed off the details that she fed me about him as if I didn't want to know.

Yet I did want to know; he was six weeks older than me, the eldest of seven Hankinson children. His sister Lily was the same age as our Joe. JJ had two further sisters and three brothers, and he worked as a mule piecer in The Bank Mill not far from his house. None of this information did I seek out, but I did secretly and eagerly absorb all these titbits as a small bird picks up grubs and worms from the soil.

I continued going to work in the carding room of the Ivy mill with Lizzie and Eunice. Every morning at early light we would get up, grab some bread, and troop down Wrigley Head to the Mill in our clogs to the sound of the mill whistle.

Swarms of us; men, women, young boys and girls like us, all part of the huge machine of the industry that made the mill owners rich whilst the vast majority of us slaved away five days a week from dawn until dusk. Oldham was known the world over for its cotton and that's what we were born to. Mill fodder I suppose we were. Little did I know then that my existence was dependent upon cotton and the slave trade in the West Indies. I didn't even question it. Thousands of people, interdependent on this vast world trade just for our daily living. Life in a northern mill town was so reliant upon a huge global exchange of life and work for the end product - Cotton. From slavery to slaving for a pittance that only just got families through the week. Slaves we all were, from top to bottom, day to day, week to week.

I felt grateful that I had earned enough to help Ma feed us all, and by saving a little each week, I managed to buy myself some new brown boots that laced up the front and had a little heel. They were only for best I promised myself.

And I often thought about JJ. He too was a part of the huge machine, a small cog, just in another mill. Me in one mill at the beginning of the process of combing the raw cotton to be spun; he in another, working on the spinning mules that spun that cotton into thread. Each mill competing to produce the best cotton they could.

And so, the months passed, and Lizzie had made sure that JJ and I crossed paths as often as she could manipulate.

The first time I ever spoke to him was just after Christmas. She had organised for Alex to meet her with JJ when she knew I would be with her. He and I were both awkward and shy.

He was quite softly spoken and slightly taller than me. He had a very kind, yet simple and innocent face with a crop of light brown hair, similar in colour to my own. He had combed it back from his forehead but a lock of it sprang forwards in a charming way, curling just above his left eye. He shuffled about consciously as he knew as well as I did that Lizzie and Alex had set us both up.

I looked up at him, a quick glance at first but he hadn't noticed. The second time I looked he was looking straight at me, and our eyes met. My eyes were brown and his, a light blue with a depth I couldn't fathom. I stepped towards him and blinked with the shock as if I had been stung. Quickly I stepped away and blushed again. He reached out as if to grab me and then stopped himself, our eyes still locked in astonishment at the impact of that brief moment.

"S... sorry," he stuttered. "I didn't mean to surprise you."

"It's alright," I replied, quickly looking away and down at the ground. "It's alright, you didn't," I said again.

"Should we walk?" he asked, and I meekly nodded my reply.

We stepped out together trying to keep a distance yet both of us must have felt the same. I knew I was smitten. My heart was pounding in my chest and my lips were dry.

It felt like a very long time before we spoke again, our first words were stilted and we were both tongue-tied, but soon enough we both eased and within half an hour we were chatting away and laughing together as if we had known each other for years. We liked the same books, and both showed an interest in nature. Strangely we had both enjoyed walking by the canal although our paths had never crossed before. We discussed the changing of the seasons, the flowers and the trees, the birds and insects and we each learned that our favourite flower was honesty. The deep purple flowers and the pretty seedpods that looked like pennies with a silvery see-through membrane once the seeds had ripened and the outer pod could be peeled away. JJ told me the seeds could be eaten. They tasted like mustard he said and the leaves taste of cabbage. We both laughed at that as we neither particularly liked cabbage nor could we imagine wanting to eat the leaves of honesty.

"I have some dried honesty in a pot in my bedroom," I offered. "Lizzie, Eunice and I grow it on Ma's allotment and peel back the seed pod so that we can see the silvery part. They make a nice arrangement."

The afternoon was cold and there had been a frost that morning. In the shadows and dark places, the silvery frost remained yet I felt warm. My feet were cold in my boots, my face cold from the frosty air, but there was a warm glow that evening, deep within me. An inner heat that made me smile and secretly wish I could reach out to touch him as we walked back towards South View where we said our tentative goodbyes.

I watched him and Alex walk away from Lizzie and me. She turned to go inside but I watched the two boys from the alley way as they went down Ellesmere Street, each with a spring in their step, playfully punching each other's arms, teasing each other's elation. I smiled again to myself and followed Lizzie inside, running up upstairs to take off my smart new boots.

"You look happy, Beatrice," Ma had stated that first evening when I had come home with my cheeks flushed and a special smile on my face. "Did you enjoy your walk with Lizzie and Alex?"

"Oh, Ma!" I answered, breathless and animated. We were drying the pots together after tea; the others were sat in front of the fire, keeping warm.

"I met Alex's friend and we all walked together. He's called John James, JJ for short and we got on well. He's so nice," I added dreamily.

Ma smiled at me with a perceptive smile. A sweet smile, filled with love, compassion and knowing. She knew how I felt; I had seen the same look on her face when she had fallen in love with Joe, our Pa. That inexplicable feeling of youthful love in its bud, a tiny flower just waiting to unfurl its petals to bloom and give joy to all those who see it.

"Oh Ma," I sighed again.

"Get away with you!" she laughed, taking the cloth from my hand and the plate I was supposed to be drying. "You'll rub the pattern off!"

I looked forward to summer that year with added anticipation and I wasn't disappointed. We met whenever we could, whenever Ma said it was all right to of course. We walked and we talked for hours. We shared our likes and dislikes and found they were so very similar.

As spring turned to summer, my sixteenth birthday swiftly approached, and I asked if we could go to Boggart Hole Clough for a family picnic as we used to when we were small. I also asked if John could perhaps come with us too. His birthday had been on the 8th May and yet he said that his family didn't do much in the way of celebrating birthdays. I asked him if it was because his parents hadn't lost any children, but he said they had.

"Only two months ago my little sister Emily died." He said sorrowfully. "She was only two."

"Oh, I'm sorry John," I replied, reaching out and touching his arm, "Why didn't you say anything?"

"My Mam won't talk about it, and we are not allowed to either," he answered, and so the matter was closed.

We try to celebrate our survival I suppose. Many families understand loss, as we did, but perhaps they didn't realise that we were all survivors on the sea of life. Time together is precious, and we are not all so lucky to have that.

I half expected Ma to say no, but to my surprise, she agreed. Alex was invited too, and I glided along upon a cloud that day. This year we packed a large picnic with plenty of food, drinks and tasty things. We had some early tomatoes from the allotment too and freshly boiled eggs. Eunice had helped Ma to make some buns.

The buns tasted even better this year than I ever remembered them tasting before. Memories flooded back of the time our Pa, had pushed Minnie in her pram up the steep hill and, as sad as we were to have lost her, we tried to be happy to remember those we had lost; including Pa who was always so very much on our minds and in our hearts.

Later that year, I recall it being early autumn. Eunice and I were lying in bed chatting. Whispering to each other as only sisters do, worried they might be overheard by Ma and told to go to sleep.

"Can you smell something funny, Beatrice?" asked Eunice.

"No?" I sniffed the air. I could smell the damp of the air; I could smell autumn. The damp sooty smell from the fire downstairs, banked up for the night so that it would burn slowly and still be in the next morning, ready for the day's cooking. All familiar, normal smells to me.

"What can you smell?" I asked her.

"I don't know," she sniffed again. "It smells fresh, no, smoky. Fresh smoky," she said, sitting up in bed to sniff again.

"It's the fire downstairs, I just heard Ma stoke it up ready for the night," I said sleepily. "Stop worrying."

"No," she persisted. "It's not that kind of smell." She climbed over me and out of bed. She fumbled about in the candlelight looking for her knitted socks to keep her feet warm.

I sat up, now sniffing the air to try to understand what she could smell that was different to normal. As she slowly opened the bedroom door, I could smell it. A burning aroma and quite different to the fire downstairs.

"It's coming from Joe's room!" she exclaimed in a hushed hoarse whisper. "Look, smoke coming from under the door and a light flickering, that's more than a candle, Beatrice!"

She climbed the wooden steps up to Joe's room and hastily opened the door.

She stifled a squeal and dashed in. I was up behind her at the door now and watched through the smoke and flames in horror as she grabbed the pitcher of water off Joe's nightstand and threw the whole lot at Joe and the smouldering blanket on his bed where his cigarette had landed as he fell asleep with it in his hand.

He woke with a start.

"What the...!" he yelled. "Eunice! What? What did you do that for? I'm all wet!"

"Better than burning in your bed Joe. What are you thinking?" she shouted as she dragged the blankets off him, stamping on them to smother the remaining flames. "You are ten years old! Smoking in bed! You could have burned the house down!"

Chapter fifteen

Ringlets

I stood with my face in my hands, frozen to the spot, mouth open wide in a half scream. I sensed rather than heard Ma behind me and Lizzie at the foot of the steps behind her.

"What the devil is going on?" demanded Ma, her voice high pitched in shock and horror of the sight that was in front of her.

Joe didn't answer but Eunice most certainly did.

"I smelled smoke Ma, I got up to investigate and there was smoke coming under Joe's door and a flickering. I threw water on him to put the fire out!" she shouted. "Silly boy was smoking in bed!" She pushed past Ma and me and burst into tears as she climbed back down the loft steps and ran into our bedroom.

I was torn between going to Joe, who stood dripping wet by his bed, or going to my little sister in her distress. Such a lot had happened, and she was such a sensitive soul. She took everything to heart and had only just got over Joe almost drowning in the canal two years ago and the rabbits escaping last year. I never dared to tell her that it had been Lizzie who let them out; she would have been so much more upset.

Lizzie turned immediately and followed Eunice into our room to comfort her. Ma passed me, immobile in the doorway to inspect the damage. I half expected her to lift her arm and box Joe's ears but instead, she gathered her boy up into her arms, as wet as he was and kissed his head.

"Eye lad, you silly boy," she said under her breath. "Oh, you silly, silly boy."

"I'm sorry Ma," that was all he said. "I'm sorry Ma."

I managed to move. First to pull the singed wet blankets off his bed and then to burst into tears myself. Ma reached out and pulled me to her too. We stood there in our nightclothes and Joe in his underpants and flat cap, while Eunice sobbed, on our bed in the arms of Lizzie.

Eventually, we all calmed down and Ma found another blanket for Joe. We had to haul his mattress over so that it was dry for him to sleep on and finally we all managed to get back into our own beds. I lay with Eunice gently snoring in my arms, her blonde curls splayed out over the pillow and warm on my shoulder. I lay staring at the ceiling for a long time before I finally drifted off to sleep.

Needless to say, Ma watched Joe like a hawk over the next few weeks and he was very compliant. Docile, sweet and kind he was, our sweet little brother.

Little devil!

"Come on Lizzie, hurry up, we'll be late." stressed Eunice as she shouted up the stairs to Lizzie and me. She had been given a prize for sitting an examination at the New Jerusalem Chapel on Oldham Road and we were going to the prize giving which was being held in Manchester. She had been ready for over an hour, but Lizzie was taking as long as she could to get ready.

Ma hadn't felt well for a few days and decided to stay at home with Joe, so we three girls were allowed to go alone.

I came down the stairs with my new boots on and my best dress and new woollen shawl. It had been very cold all week and there were reports it might snow before Christmas. We had a nice enough summer I suppose although the snows in January this year had been very heavy and deep. We were all hoping that we wouldn't have to endure the same this winter.

Finally, we were all ready and set off, wrapped up against the cold. Our shawl covered heads down, arms folded across our chests, hands wrapped within our shawls. The three of us, now young ladies, marching quickly against the icy wind, we crossed over the road and over to Oldham Road where we boarded an electric tram that would take us into Manchester.

Every other time I had ever been in Manchester, I had been with Ma, a child in the care of an adult. Scurrying along behind her, trying to keep up and not truly looking at the world around me. This time it struck me that I was now grown up and I looked at everything with fresh eyes.

I gazed through the window with renewed excitement as the tram clattered out of Failsworth, past the gloomy mills and dark towering mill chimneys; through Newton Heath, past the tanneries and brickworks, Monsal, Miles Platting and the railway foundries, ironworks and railway sidings and on through Ancoats where Ma's family used to live when she was younger; the rows upon rows of tightly packed streets of houses, slums and back to backs where children in rags and tatters sat on doorsteps in the cold afternoon air as if it were summertime, their frail pinched faces watching us go by.

The poor unsanitary housing finally gave way to massive red brick and creamy Cheshire stone-fronted ornate buildings as we arrived in Piccadilly Square and alighted the tram. Five and six-storey office buildings soared above me, ornately carved stonework with turrets adorning the corners. Elegant, polished brass company plaques and shiny doorknobs on stylish oak entrance doors, reflecting the wealth of the business and trading companies that owned them. Wealth accumulated on the backs and strife of the poor families living in the very slums we had just passed, and the hard work of the men and women employed in the industries I had just seen on my journey. The blood, sweat and tears of the people, slaving away for a pittance had grown this wealth and accumulated fortunes for the few men at the top.

Those poor people, trapped into a life of poverty, their only escape, alcohol or death. Such a sad and vicious circle of hard toil, deprivation, hunger and destitution, leading to riches for the company owners and desperation for the expendable workers; driving some of them to alcoholism, violence and yet more poverty. I had seen it in my own family and my own town so many times that it seemed normal. I now saw the other end of the scale, here in the corporate hub, the prosperity and grandeur of the beautiful city of Manchester.

We crossed over the road to Piccadilly gardens and in front of us towered the huge sculpture of the dead Queen of our great Empire that they had unveiled just over ten years ago. Six huge steps led up to an oversized bronze statue of Queen Victoria in her dotage, seated on her throne, wearing an enormous lace dress and holding her sceptre and orb. Above her on the marble plinth was also a bronze figure of St George fighting the dragon.

"Come on," insisted Eunice. "Come on."

We hurried down Mossley Street following her, turning left and right again, getting confused until we managed to find the hall we were looking for. I was glad Eunice knew where we were going as I had to admit that I was totally disoriented, and I clung to Lizzie's hand as tightly as I could for fear I were to get lost.

We entered the huge ornately decorated entrance hall through the most beautiful polished wooden double doors. Mosaic tiled flooring and marble columns surrounded us, polished oak balustrades and a colossal staircase rose in front of us. We held our breaths in awe as we entered the huge room where the presentation was to take place and found our seats from the seating plan that Eunice held tightly in her hand.

Smartly suited men in tall hats gave speeches, with golden watch chains draped from their waistcoats. Large trophies were given out to pompous well-dressed dignitaries. Eventually, the clapping subsided and our leader, Mr Pinney took to the stage. He gave a short speech, the contents of which made little sense to us, but he then started to call out the names of people that were more familiar to me.

"Miss Eunice Humphreys," he announced in his booming authoritative voice. "One hundred and twenty-six marks. First Class in the National Examinations. Well done, Eunice."

She stood up and shot an excited look at us both proudly making her way to the front and up onto the stage to collect her prize of a small brown hard backed book appropriately entitled 'A self-willed family.'

She was so proud of that book and read it from cover to cover within a week. Every night when she came home from work, she picked up her precious book; she read it out loud and then again quietly to herself, over and over.

"The girl's surname is Marshall," she explained again to our patient Ma. Their mother had died………"

"Oh, not again Eunice, please," groaned Joe. "I've heard the story ten times already." He rolled about on the floor with his hands over his ears.

"The woman in charge of the spinning loom I work on is called Mrs Marshall." She replied, ignoring Joe. "Isn't that a coincidence? I don't like her at all. She pushes me and the other girls about and shouts all the time." She added to herself, becoming absorbed once again in her book.

As it turned out, a few months later and well after Christmas that year, I met Mrs Marshall. She was a formidable woman, thin and wiry with a pointed nose and chin.

I had been for a walk over to the cemetery with John and as we turned into Ellesmere Street, she almost bumped into me as she walked briskly with her head down, not watching where she was going. She grunted as I stepped aside for her to pass.

That was the first time I saw her; then again in May about a week after John's birthday. She scowled at me coming out of the factory gates as I waited for Eunice on the corner where I usually wait for her and the girl who live next door to us, Janie Melling. Janie worked with Eunice and although she was ten years older, the two got on well.

"That's her," whispered Eunice from behind me, she poked me and pointed in Mrs Marshall's direction. "Bitter old goat!" she added with a laugh.

Janie Melling and Eunice linked arms with me, and we fell into step together on the way home.

The third time I encountered Mrs Marshall was in the middle of June, the week before my 19th birthday, when I was sent to work on the same floor as Eunice. There had been an influx of new young girls and the foreman in the carding room decided that they should all start work there and a few of us were sent upstairs to the spinning floor to make way for them.

The clattering and noise was deafening and I waved at Eunice as I spotted her a few looms behind me. Her red headscarf was a flash of colour amid the choking heat and dust of the huge and noisy room. I was set to work instantly by a small man who only had one arm. He nodded to me and gestured above the din.

"Fetch those spindles, be quick girl" he mouthed, flinging his one arm and pointing to a large wooden truck full of empty spindles. I looked around and took four empty spindles out of the truck, handing them to him. He deftly placed them onto the machine rack.

"Ta," he mouthed above the din. Then he waved his arm impatiently and nodded at me to get some more for him. He showed me how to mount each one onto the frame and then how to catch the thread and feed the cotton onto each spindle. I was amazed at how fast he worked and with only one arm.

I was taller than him and could reach higher up and so he ordered me to continue where he left off. The cotton yarn spun around and quickly filled the spindles; then I had to take the full spindles off, place them into another cart and a young boy with bare feet wheeled it away. The whole process repeated, and I was alarmed just how quickly I needed to work to change the full spindles with the empty ones, repeatedly. Such speed, I could hardly keep up!

Occasionally the cotton thread snapped, and he showed me how to catch the thread and to fasten the ends again to continue the process.

I didn't have much time to look up but when I did, I saw Eunice once again, but this time she was across the passageway to the side of me working on another row of spinning machines like mine.

Mrs Marshall was stood doing the very job I had been tasked to do, although I noticed that she was so much faster than I was, her wiry fingers catching up the cotton and deftly making the whole machine run much more smoothly than I did.

Eunice and Janie were kneeling on the floor picking up any dropped spindles, catching fluff and other debris that had fallen underneath. I don't know why I watched Eunice but I couldn't look away. It was as if I was waiting for something to happen.

Time stood still; I could no longer hear the machines whirring. My hands reached out towards Eunice, and I watched in horror as Mrs Marshall pushed Janie, angrily telling both girls to get further down under the machines. Janie tried to stand up but with her hand on Eunice's back, she accidently pushed Eunice down and further under the machine.

Her red headscarf caught on something above her as she screamed. Her hair, her beautiful ringlets caught in the workings. I leapt across the space between us to my sister. I dived under the machine, not caring about myself or the cotton or the spindles. I felt myself drag her little body to me and I cradled her gently as I felt her slump in my arms.

A huge clump of hair had been ripped from her head and her pretty face was starting to swell up. I heard a loud shout and scream that came from deep inside me.

She blinked and looked up at me, trembling as two larger men dragged me to a standing position and another took Eunice from me. I followed them as they whisked Eunice away from the spinning machines and downstairs and out into the yard.

"Which way love?" asked the man carrying Eunice.

"South View," I answered as I reached out to hold her dangling hand. She had fainted again.

Joe was on his way home from school and ran over to me as he saw the man carrying Eunice.

"Run home Joe," I begged him. I was in tears now, horrified at what I had seen happen to my baby sister. "Run home and tell Ma to get the doctor. There's been an accident!"

He started to ask questions, but I pushed him away and he ran, faster than I've ever seen him run, across Wrigley Head and home to tell Ma that our poor Eunice was hurt.

Chapter sixteen

The Infirmary

Ma was at the door as we arrived home and Joe had been sent to fetch the doctor. The man carrying Eunice followed Ma up the stairs into the bedroom where he laid her gently down on our bed.

"I'll be off then," he mumbled, removing his cap, and nodding to Ma. "Hope she'll be alright Missus."

"Thank you," Ma answered, not looking up. She straightened Eunice's dress and gently stroked her pale swollen face with her hand.

As the man left, Lizzie and Elsie Haslem, Eunice's long-time friend, dashed up the stairs together. They had heard that Eunice had been hurt and had run home together as soon as they could get off work, leaving Janie Melling in tears after apparently being blamed for the whole disaster by Mrs Marshall even though it was an accident by all accounts.

Poor Janie.

"Beatrice, fetch some cool boiled water and a clean cloth." Ma said. There was a calm look on her face despite the concern in her eyes. I returned as soon as I could, and Ma started to bathe her daughter's face and the patch of skin where her beautiful hair had been ripped out.

Little spots of blood were starting to show on her scalp just under her skin. Her right eye was swollen and looked blue, the start of what would prove to be a large black eye by morning.

She stirred and looked up at Ma's smiling face. "Ma. I'm hurt," she said in a meek small voice.

"I know love, the Doctor will be here soon."

"My throat hurts too," Eunice added, putting her hand to her throat and coughing. "I haven't been able to sing."

"It does look a little swollen," Ma confirmed, touching Eunice's neck herself. We could all now see a swelling just left of centre.

"It's been getting worse all summer, but I thought it would go better so I didn't say anything about it," she said in a rather croaky voice.

Just then Joe arrived back with the Doctor. He went straight upstairs, and we all came away leaving Ma with Eunice and Doctor Taylor.

Some ten minutes later when they came back down, he confirmed to us all that Eunice was suffering from shock and would have bruising to her head. She was to rest quietly and only time would tell as to whether her hair would grow back.

"A more concerning thing however is her throat," he said with a troubled look on his face. "I suspect she might have an Exophthalmic Goitre. I will make enquiries and see if we can get her to Manchester Infirmary, they have been carrying out trials of a new treatment with iodine and I think it may help."

There was a silence and Ma sat down heavily on the rocking chair, bursting into tears. Lizzie placed a comforting hand on her shoulder and handed her a handkerchief.

"Thank you, Doctor," she sniffed. "What will happen to my poor child?"

"I will be in touch," he stated in a matter-of-fact tone. As if this was not that worrisome and silly women crying didn't help the matter. He turned to go, placing his top hat on his head, nodding and leaving us all aghast with the situation.

Apart from us having to hold Joe back from going to thump Janie Melling and Mrs Marshall, we spent the next couple of weeks carefully tending to Eunice. After a few days of bed rest, she felt well enough to sit up and even to come downstairs for a few hours in the evening to eat. Once or twice venturing outside to look at the rabbits.

Dusty and Willow had been long gone but we now had two breeding females, Agatha and Dottie and one buck called, Mr Bramble. Where Joe dreamed up those names, I will never know but he always made us laugh with the serious look on his face when he arrived at his decisions. There was always a naming ceremony and a blessing too and we all had to stifle our giggles and keep a straight face for the occasion.

On Friday, 10th July, an official letter arrived with an invite for Eunice to go to Manchester Royal Infirmary the following Monday morning where she would receive experimental treatment for her goitre. Joe's twelfth birthday went uncelebrated this year as poor Eunice took centre stage.

Lizzie and I were in work; Joe was in school, and Ma took Eunice to Chorlton-on-Medlock to the hospital. When we finished our shifts, we hurried home and set about asking Ma hundreds of questions.

"Yes, Eunice is alright; yes, she's in good hands; yes, I met her doctor; yes, they said she will be home in about three weeks; yes, they will feed her; yes, she can have visitors in a week or so," answered Ma to each of our demands. "She'll be fine, I'm sure," she added as she busied herself making tea and setting the table.

Life without Eunice in the house was very strange. Looking back, we realised that we hadn't heard her singing for the last few weeks, she'd been quiet, and she had taken to wearing a scarf around her neck.

"She was hiding it wasn't she?" I whispered to Lizzie, out of earshot of Ma and Joe.

"I suppose she was," she whispered back. "She must have been quite worried and didn't know what to do, poor love."

That night in my bed I realised that for the very first time in my life I was in bed alone; without any sister or brother with me, entirely alone and it felt very strange indeed.

I stretched out my foot a little to where I usually felt Eunice's leg.

I turned myself over to where her head was usually on the pillow next to mine.

I listened in the darkness for her breathing.

Before I fell asleep, I whispered, "God Bless Eunice."

I waited for her to answer in the silence.

Over the next few days, so many people came to call and to ask after Eunice.

The Melling's; Janie's family from next door; and kind Mrs Borwick from the other side. Mrs

Nixon and Nellie, who Eunice also worked with, came over to see Ma as did Mrs Ashton who came several times every week anyway. Everyone in the street who knew us sent their good wishes and asked us to send love to Eunice.

"She's in Bridgewater Ward, M4 females," Ma was telling Mrs Lane and Mrs Clough, who had stopped by one afternoon and were talking to Ma on our doorstep.

"We can't go in to see her yet but I'm sure she would be happy to receive a postcard from you." Ma said. Happy with that they went on their way and Elsie and I followed Ma into the house.

"That's a good idea," said Elsie. "I will pop to the shop to buy a postcard to send to Eunice. I'm sure it will cheer her up. Are you coming, Beatrice?"

We walked together to the little shop where they sold lots of everything including postcards and I helped Elsie to pick out a nice card to send to Eunice. There was a coloured picture of a girl on the front wearing a green knitted hat and a pink dress.

"Perfect," smiled Elsie as she handed over her money to Mrs Pillkington. I decided that I would write a letter later, but Elsie immediately took the card back home to our house and wrote:

*E. Haslam 453 Manchester Road Hollinwood
Nr Oldham
Dear Eunice, Just a line hoping you are feeling a
little better, pluck up and then you will be better
sooner. I will come and see you as soon as I can.
With best of love and xxxxxxx from Elsie*

By the time we got to visit Eunice, she had quite a collection of good wishes on postcards from many of her friends and neighbours. All very nice and positive cards and they all said how much they wished she was getting better and that she would come home soon. There was even one from Joe, that I hadn't even realised he had sent.

I picked it up and took a seat on a hard wooden chair at the foot of her hospital bed. It was a colourful postcard from Failsworth with picture of a basket of flowers on it. The words on the front said:

*A loving wish from Failsworth
Just a greeting loyal and true
A message sweet and kind
To prove though out of sight of you
You are not out of mind*

*"Dear Sister
I am writing these lines hoping to see you soon.
As we are thinking of you. Hoping to see you*

well and in good health when I come as I am
feeling lonely.
From your loving brother Joe."
xxxx

"Oh, Joe, that's really sweet," I said to him, he sat down on the edge of the bed beside our sick sister.

The card that I had sent to her was there too.

With love and best wishes from Failsworth.

A picture of some wood violets printed on the front, and I had written on the back,

> *Dearest Sister*
> *I hope you will take notice of the words and that*
> *you will cheer up. I have been longing to see you*
> *and would have come today but sister says we are*
> *not to come yet. But you will see by this that you*
> *are not forgotten.*
> *With best love, Beatrice.*
> *xxxxxx.*

We clearly all missed her very much and all hoped she was getting better, and that the treatment was going to work, but she looked pale and wan. Her hair had lost its shine and her face its natural glow. She looked very poorly indeed.

I met up with John a few days later and although sympathetic to hear about Eunice, he was strangely excited.

"There's fighting in the Balkans," he said, smiling at my confused face.

"Where's that?" I asked with a frown. "Why are they fighting? who? who's fighting?"

"Oh Beatrice, you're such a girl," he laughed. "They shot Archduke Ferdinand and Germany, Russia and all the other countries are getting rather hot under the collar about it. Some say there'll be a war and the newspapers say that Britain will doubtless mobilise should war begin. Isn't it exciting Beatrice?"

"No! No, it isn't," I said in disgust. I disagreed and he laughed at my protestations as we walked along the canal. He tried to explain the situation to me and repeating all that he had read about in the newspapers; but all I could think about was Eunice. Her tired little face and the horrid treatment she had to go through. The doctors had explained it to Ma, but we didn't understand it, nor did they even know if it would work.

We didn't know if she would come home or not, and we all missed her terribly. Joe made sure that the rabbits were well looked after and now that he was twelve, we learned that he too would join us in the mill and finish at school. He was excited to start earning money and had grand designs on how he would spend it too.

The next birthday would be Eunice's and a week before she had written a card to Lizzie to tell her that she was feeling much better.

In reply to this, and one with a Dutch girl on it that she had sent to me, I found a sweet little card to send back to her. There was photograph on the front of the Fountain at Bogart Hole Clough.

I thought about all the happy times we had spent there. From when she was only small, skipping along holding hands, the three of us, carefree and innocent to the horrors of the future. Completely unaware of what was to come.

I wanted to cheer her up and so I wrote:

> *Dear Sister*
> *I am writing to let you know that I still think of you and hope that you are still on the mend. Just think of the happy times you have spent in this place.*
> *With love from Beatrice*
> *xxxxxxxxxxxx*
> *Goodbye*

Alex and John and all their friends were following the news from abroad regarding the developing situation in Germany. Everyone was talking about it, at work and in the streets. The newsstands were full of the headlines of the day and the impending war. As John had said, it was all getting very exciting, the working men of the country were being urged join up to fight too.

The whole thing gave me an underlying sense of foreboding that always comes when the word war is mentioned.

It was only just over twelve years since the Boer War in Africa had ended and the war in the Crimea was still living memory for some older men. I remembered that Grandpa Ward had tried to tell me about it when I had still been in school and our teacher had asked us to write about it in our copybooks. I was more fascinated to learn of the work of Florence Nightingale rather than the reasons the countries were fighting. More upset that men were being hurt, wounded and killed than anything else, yet it seemed so very long ago to me as a young girl.

John came to meet me from work one warm August day just after Eunice's sixteenth birthday, with a sheet of paper in his hand. He waved it excitedly at me.

"Look Beatrice, read this," he said as he thrust the paper into my hand.

I took the newspaper sheet from his hand and read the proclamation from King George.

A shiver ran down my spine as I read out loud.

"Owing to the rejection by the German Government of the request made by his Majesty's

Government for the assurance that the neutrality of Belgium will be respected. His Majesty's Ambassador at Berlin has received his passports. His Majesty's Government have declared to the German Government that a state of war exists between Great Britain and Germany as from 11pm on August 4th."

I turned my face to him with my mouth agog and eyes wide open in astonishment.

"What does that mean John?" I asked.

"It means they want men to go and fight. Alex is going to find out how we can join up too."

"Fight!? You!?" I replied, astonished that he would even think of it. "You're too gentle John, you're not a fighter" I giggled.

He laughed but I knew he was offended.

"It's not fighting like in a pub brawl, Beatrice. We would be trained and there are guns. We must be strong against the enemy. It's a noble thing to fight for King and country."

"I just can't see you getting into a fight, that's all." I looked up at his youthful face and he met my smile with his.

Eunice finally did come home in early September. She was pale and thin, but her neck seemed less swollen, and her hair had started to grow back. Her sweet voice was weak but with all the loving care and attention, she started to get better and stronger day by day.

Her friend Elsie had been on holiday at the Wakes in August, as had Janie Melling and they had both sent postcards from Blackpool. We also found out that Mrs Borwick had also been away to Blackpool. All of them sending postcards to Eunice to say they hoped she was getting better.

Eunice unpacked her bag onto our bed and laid out all the cards from the people who wished her well. Cards with greetings from Failsworth and birthday cards too. She was quite touched by the good wishes that everyone had sent.

Janie's sister, Leah Chappell, Mr & Mrs Willisford, Mrs Link, Mrs Lane and Aunt Annie Schofield had all sent cards.

"There's a card here from Edward too. Oooo, I think you have an admirer," I teased.

"You can have these now Beatrice," she said in a sad little voice, tears dripping onto the card from Edward, smudging the ink. "Will you keep them safe for me in your box?"

I smiled at her. "Yes, if you like, I will put them in my box, and we can look at them whenever you like. One day when you're strong again we can go into Manchester and buy a little album to put them in," I promised as we gathered the cards together and placed them in my box.

That thought cheered her up and a sparkle of the old Eunice shone through. I gave her the biggest hug just as Ma shouted from downstairs.

"Elsie's here Eunice. Come down girls."

Now we were into November and her friend Elsie had been to Colwyn Bay. She sent postcards of course but as soon as she came home, she was eager to tell Eunice all about it.

Eunice sat in the rocking chair surrounded by cushions and with her knitted blanket over her knees to keep her warm. I sat at the table with my cup of tea, listening to Elsie tell Eunice all about the seaside at Colwyn Bay; the smell of the fresh breeze that blew from the sea and the bracing walks along the promenade. The view of Great Orme across the bay, the Welsh hills in the distance and the magnificent sight of Snowdon from the train. Eunice was entranced to hear all about the quaint little town of Colwyn Bay, the pier and the pavilion.

I wish you had come with me Eunice," she said, holding her best friend's hand. "We had the loveliest time; the food was delicious, and Mrs Smethers looked after us well. She's a very good cook, we had tea and cakes every afternoon. Please say you'll come next year when we go again. I saved my money in the Wakes club, and I'll put some in for you too when I get back to work."

The pair chattered away like two little old ladies, and I smiled to myself, simply happy to see my sister home once more.

Chapter seventeen

The calm before

Ma sat with Eunice for the next couple of weeks as her health slowly deteriorated. She stroked her daughter's face calmly singing to her and she lay on our bed with her day and night. She read the little book that Eunice so treasured, out loud and Eunice smiled up at her and dozed. She was getting weaker and weaker day by day, despite the food we brought her and despite the love and promises we gave her.

I slept with Lizzie in Ma's bed instead and we lay in the silence just staring at each other and trying to avoid the tears that we knew would come but were fearfully hidden. If we broke, we were beaten, and Eunice was too precious to let her go; if we cried it would be too late.

Sometimes we just stared at the ceiling, holding hands under the blankets in the darkness, the cold of the night weighing heavy on our hearts.

Joe was quiet too; he often went in to sit with Eunice to tell her how the rabbits were doing, and Eunice would smile for him as she listened to his poems and his little stories.

We had all been here too many times before. The impending loss, the approaching hurt that we knew was coming yet again to haunt us. The imminent unavoidable pain of losing someone we all loved so dearly and the unfairness of life without them.

"The world doesn't care," said Lizzie one teatime when she came in from work. "It just goes on as if nothing matters and all everyone talks about is the war. They said it would be over by Christmas but it's increasingly obvious that it won't be. It's all Alex talks about!"

She was angry, I could tell.

"Tea?" I questioned as if a cup of tea solved everything.

She nodded, a drained look on her face and sat down, on the rocking chair.

"How's Eunice?" she asked wearily.

"Not good," I answered, handing her a brew in her favourite cup. It had a chip on the rim, but she said the tea always tasted better in that cup than in any other.

Dr Taylor said it wouldn't be long now." I turned my head from her, a lump forming in my throat. I couldn't have said that while I looked into Lizzie's eyes. I would have cracked just then, but I held firm.

"Oh! I'll go up to her in a minute. She took a sip of the hot liquid. "Is there a cup of tea for her?"

"Yes," I answered, pouring one cup for Eunice and one for Ma out of the big brown teapot that was snuggly wrapped in its knitted tea cosy. Eunice had knitted it a couple of years ago and I placed my hands around it to warm them. As if that would keep her safe.

She breathed her last on the 13th of December, safely wrapped in her mother's arms, with Lizzie, Joe and me looking helplessly on.

That cold dark Sunday morning, our world just stopped revolving. The snow that had been falling for the last couple of weeks muffled every sound. Even the ticking of the clock downstairs sounded subdued; powerless to stop time.

On the Thursday, in the snow, we laid her with our Pa and the babies under the willow tree. The branches bare, the ground cold and hard and my bones ached with longing to hear her sing once more. She lay just a few yards away from our Daddy and across the little path from Granny Ward.

John stood behind me, Lizzie and Joe to my right. I looked up to see my Ma, black-veiled once more, bereft and empty.

I sank to the ground, not caring for the brown wet mud that soaked into my skirts, chilling my knees. I let the tears come at last.

Time moves on and so the world turns. Life has its ebbs and flows and the ever-changing seasons' mark time for each of us.

I remember little from the immediate period after the death of my little sister; apart from the fact that I knew it even hurt to say her name for a very long time.

I worked... I ate... I slept. I watched the trees come into bud and heard the birds calling for each other when I took my walks with John down by the canal. The barges were still heavily laden, the dirt and grime from the mills was still thick in the muggy days of June. My birthday came and went without any event apart from me receiving some lovely birthday cards. I placed them in my box without looking at the ones I knew were in there already. The ones that were supposed to bring me joy when I looked at them. The ones that I had promised her we would buy an album for to put them in together.

I have no wish to see them.

Not yet.

It was almost a year since we had celebrated Eunice's sixteenth birthday in the hospital before she came home, and I thought my heart was starting to mend a little. It was easier to remember her with fondness than with pain now, and I smiled more when I remembered her. In the quietness of the night, I could hear her whisper, her soft breathing perhaps; or was it just my imagination?

We often walked down by the canal, JJ and me. It was our favourite way along the towpath. We always took this longer route from work rather than going straight home. The way by the canal was much nicer; our time together was precious after the noise and toil of the day. We always crossed over the humpback bridge at the lock to see the house where we used to live on Alfred Street, then back again over the bridge, sometimes stopping to watch the boats go through the lock or to stop and chat with a boatman or his wife.

Today was warm and sultry and we walked slowly along the towpath as if we didn't want our walk to end. Everyone else hurried home for tea; but John and I loitered, just enjoying our time together as tired as we both were. After a while, we came to a halt underneath Wrigley Head bridge. He took my hand and stepped close to me.

A ray of sunlight shone down onto the surface of the water of the canal. A barge had just gone past and the ripples of the wake from it glittered with the golden sunlight, reflecting the movement onto the stones of the underside of the bridge. The water looked quite clear, and I saw through the water to the bottom of the canal, reeds swaying and little fish motionless in that one solitary moment of a sunbeam.

"It's not very deep, is it?" I mused.

"What isn't?" he replied, catching my gaze and looking deep into my eyes.

"The water… It's shallower than I thought."

He didn't answer. He simply looked into my eyes, and I could feel the warmth of his body, closer to me than we had ever been before. I looked up at him and slowly closed my eyes. His kiss on my cheek was as soft as a white swan's feather, pure and clean. His next kiss landed gently on my waiting lips. I drank in the smell of him; the warmth of the moment filled my soul as I felt his soft kiss linger on my lips.

Slowly, so slowly I opened my eyes as the moment dissolved and our kiss melted into the past. Neither of us spoke, we were lost in each other's eyes.

"I wanted to kiss you since I first saw you." He whispered.

I don't know how we got home that evening, how I ate my tea or how I finally managed to climb wearily into my bed. I could still feel his lips on mine, and I didn't want to lose that sensation. Ma had said how quiet I was; I hadn't answered her; that way his touch stayed with me.

Many, many kisses we shared in the next few weeks and months. Secret, warm and tender. I felt my heart would burst until he kissed me again. We hurried towards the bridge on those days when his shift allowed him to meet me, and we could spend our secret time under the bridge together.

I quite forgot how shocked I had been when Lizzie and Alex were getting a little too close a couple of years ago. That didn't matter to me now.

Now I was in the middle of it myself.

The careless run towards adulthood that comes to every young girl, when her heart sings, her emotions fly, and her body resonates with pure joy.

Only once did we ever get seen kissing. My head was resting on his chest, his arm around my shoulders as the evenings got darker and the weather began to turn colder. A whistle from a man on a passing barge as he caught sight of our shadow, our two bodies so close together that he had realised what he thought was one man, was the two of us in a tender embrace.

Even on the warmest days, there are clouds; in joy a there is an aching; when all feels well with the world there appears a smudge in the distance as if time is pausing; delaying, before taking away the peace. Waiting for the bad that must come.

Conscription came in the new year of 1916. My handsome JJ was called up to go and join the army. He was only nineteen and was enlisted into the 27th Manchester Regiment. They were a reservist regiment, and he would be leaving Failsworth for Southport where he said he would be training. He looked so smart in his uniform, proud and strong. The boy I fell in love with was now a soldier, a man.

"Private Hankinson 28974," he proudly said when I next saw him. "I'm off to Southport for training."

"Will you go and fight in France?" I asked him, worried that he would be going away from me and yet proud that he would be playing his part in the fight against the German advance.

"I'll write, often," he promised as he boarded the train, blowing a kiss to me from his fingertips. I reached up to catch it in the air, waving my handkerchief as the train pulled slowly away from the station. I stood on the platform with other girls my age and mothers of boys, all proudly waving and cheerily saying our goodbyes. Watching him go with a mixture of emotions churning in my head, and in my stomach.

His sister Elizabeth wrote to him where he was lodging with his company at 83 London Street

Southport, and he sent a photograph of his company outside the house.

His letter was short and didn't tell me very much. His landlady was Mrs Holmes, and the food was alright, he said. He would be going to a training camp near Liverpool and life in the army didn't seem too bad. He said he was having fun, training and learning how to be a soldier.

In the May I received word that he was to go to France, and he sent me some beautifully embroidered silk postcards. He knew I would treasure them. One embroidered with 'Forget me not' on the front.

He wrote on the back and my heart skipped a beat as I read.

> *Yesterday 20/5/16*
> *My dear sweetheart,*
> *We have arrived safe and sound in France and we are doing well, and brother is keeping with me, and we have had some fun so I will send a letter with my address on later so goodnight and God Bless you.*
> *From your loving sweetheart John Jas xxxxxxx*

He sent many silk cards, with flowers and flags of Britain and France; another with flowers and the words 'Heaps of Kisses for my Darling' embroidered on it.

On another card he had taken the time to spell out in little kisses, the words,

'To Beatrice from John with love.'

Another embroidered with 'Greetings from the trenches', and the words:

> *To Beatrice Humphreys from John J Hankinson with the best of love.*

He wrote to give me his address and I sent him letters and cards in return. Simple printed cards with lovely words written on them, all of them praying that God would keep him safe from harm for me.

In the August of that year, he was safely back home again after training in France. He wouldn't tell me what he had done or what fighting was like, but I wasn't concerned about that. He was home and I was a happier girl for that. He was sent back to the training camp in Altcar near Southport, apparently not needed at the front just yet. My relief was palpable, and for the time being my love was safe.

I took the train to go over to Altcar to see him, he stood on the platform waiting for me as I arrived at the station.

He looked so smart in his uniform, and I swooned to see him. I carefully climbed down from the train steps, and he held out his hand to me to help me down. He took the small bag I had with me, not letting go of my hand as we walked.

"Are you well Beatrice?" he asked, looking concerned. "You look a little peaky."

"I'm fine," I answered, looking up at him, he seemed a little older, more confident somehow. "Just excited to see you. I have really missed you." I hoped I hadn't embarrassed myself by admitting that to him, but I needed him to know. He had been away all summer and I thought about him every day. Sometimes at night, I couldn't get to sleep for the very thought of him.

"Let's go to get a cup of tea. I've lots to tell you and something to ask you too. Ma and Lily came over to see me last week, did they tell you?"

"Yes, I saw Lily and Elizabeth yesterday, and your Ma. She looked well for her holiday," I replied, squeezing his hand as he marched me out of the station and down the street towards the nearest tea house.

The air was clear and cleaner than in Failsworth. The sea air made breathing easier and the light brighter. The day was sunny and warm. We took our seats and ordered tea and cake, which was swiftly delivered by a young girl in a little white apron and starched white lace cap. John took the lead and poured a cup of tea for us both and handed me a plate with a cherry bun on it.

He looked into my eyes as I took the plate. My heart fluttered again.

"I have missed you too Beatrice," he said. His look was one full of longing and sweetness and happiness. " You know you're my sweetheart, don't you? I do so love you, Beatrice."

"Oh John," I replied as I took the little plate from him, and time stood still again. I longed to kiss him, right there in full view of the whole world.

"Marry me, Beatrice. Please be my wife."

Chapter eighteen

Mr & Mrs JJ Hankinson

Church bells usually have an unnerving way of setting off butterflies in my stomach, the fluttering and excitement, glee for the happy couple, a jittery feeling of anticipation and delight. Except we are at war and the bells of St John's couldn't ring today, I still feel the elation as if they were ringing very loud for the whole world to hear.

For today I am the bride, and the words of Aunt Annie came back to me from when I was ten years old, "happiness makes you beautiful," she had said, and I feel just so beautiful today on the arm of Mr Ashton. My Grandpa Ward had sadly passed away that July, before he had the chance to see me wed, in fact before he even knew I would be. So, Ma's friend's husband, James Ashton was pleased to stand for me.

"I would be honoured, love," he had said when I asked him, a huge look of pride on his face. "Truly honoured."

I entered the church and stopped for a moment to pinch myself so that I knew it was real. Organ music swelled and resounded in my ears, starting the jitters once more. Mr Ashton squeezed my hand and we walked slowly down the aisle, followed by Lizzie as my matron of honour, until I stood next to my handsome soldier. I peeped up at him and his eyes met mine.

Lizzie took my posy of late summer flowers and silver honesty pods from me, and I sailed on a cloud for the rest of the service and all through the afternoon. I banished sadness from my thoughts; for today I was happy.

It was a cool day, but I was warm with pleasure. The leaves had started to fall from the trees, and they whirled around us like confetti in the wind. Joe scooped up some dry ones and threw handfuls of them over us in the churchyard, under the lych-gate before we headed home for tea and cake.

Finally, John and I were alone. I removed my hat and sat on the side of the bed starting to pull the pins from my hair. John stood before the mirror and was unbuttoning his uniform while looking at my reflection behind him.

"I love you, Beatrice,"

"I love you too, didn't we have a lovely day," I replied brightly, meeting his gaze in the mirror.

"I shall remember this day when I have to go back to camp, and who knows, then over to the front."

"Shhhhh," I whispered. My heart was pounding in my chest, and I barely heard my voice above the roar in my ears. "Don't spoil it."

He turned to put his jacket on the back of the chair and came over to me. He reached over to take my hand, where he chastely placed a kiss. He then helped me to take down my hair. I let his fingers find the pins and my hair cascaded to my shoulders. I started to brush it and then plait it with my fingers. He stopped me.

"Leave it down," he said, his voice soft yet strong. He leaned forwards to kiss me. With his one hand beside me supporting himself, he placed the other hand behind my head, and he guided me backwards onto the bed, his lips still on mine, and I welcomed his weight upon me.

Just before dawn, he turned over in the bed towards me. I was facing the wall in the little room, and I could feel the warmth of his chest on my back. He tucked his knees behind mine; I smiled a secret smile to myself, pretending to still be sleeping. He lifted my hair from my shoulders and gently kissed the nape of my neck; his hand softly stroked from my bare shoulder, down to my waist and over my hips. We moved together and he tenderly loved me once more.

"Today we're going into Manchester," he announced over a breakfast of toast, eggs and tea.

"Oh, why?" I asked, blowing the heat away over the rim of my teacup and looking up at him stood warming himself on the fire, his hands clasped behind his back, the confident proud stance of a man that finally has it all.

"I have a need to spend some of my army pay on my beautiful wife," he smiled. "I always wanted to buy a gramophone. So, we can listen to music and dance together. Should we?" I giggled as he reached over to take my hand, pulling me to my feet and holding me around the waist with his right arm, in a dance hold. He started to move and dance with me.

Oh! how I loved this man and his boyish ways, his strength, his warmth and the adoring look in his eyes. I swayed with him, moving my feet with his in time to an imaginary music that played only for us.

"What you wish husband mine," I answered smiling again at his eager face. "A day in Manchester sounds nice. I should like to spend your army pay on a beautiful piano. Let me pop upstairs to get my hat and coat." I held out my skirt and bobbed a little curtsey as our dance ended, and he nodded a bow back to me.

Half an hour later we were on the tram, and I held his hand all the way to Manchester, pointing out the stop where we always got off when visiting Ma's brother, Uncle Joseph and Aunt Jane in Ancoats.

We dismounted in Stephenson Square, and I linked my husband's arm as we crossed over to Piccadilly and walked past the statue of Queen Victoria. I stopped to look up at it again and thought of the afternoon we had spent at the prize giving when Eunice received her book. This time I smiled with the memory, and we walked on down Mosley Street turning right into Princess Street. We detoured into Albert Square so that John could show me the Town Hall, as I had never seen it before, stopping to admire the beautiful building before continuing along John Dalton Street to Deansgate. Without pausing, John marched me directly into Forsyth's Music shop.

"Why are we here?" I whispered to John as we entered. The shop was cool and had a sombre feel to it. A deep red carpet felt soft underfoot and there was a huge grand piano in front of us; black and polished to a deep shine, it's top lifted open to show the soundboard and strings on the bridge. I could see all the little tuning pins, the action frame, each little hammer and the soft velvet covered dampers. I reached lovingly out to touch the keyboard, my fingers brushing them and yet not making a sound, so soft was my caress.

A smartly dressed young man approached, his head aloof; pince-nez spectacles balanced on his long thin pointy nose.

"My wife would like to look at piano's," John said confidently to him as I shyly stood a little behind him.

The man looked us both up and down slowly, from the floor to our hats, peering down his nose and turning away, beckoning with his long thin finger. "Certainly sir, Come this way."

I didn't like the condescending expression on his face; maybe he thought John was not a soldier as he wasn't in his uniform today. It was considered that you were a coward if you didn't go to fight. I didn't like this man's attitude and I scowled. My husband is a soldier I silently defended. He is brave and he is noble; and he's all mine, I thought proudly to myself.

We followed the man to the back of the shop where he rhymed off the attributes of each piano, the prices and what quality of sound we could expect. I was completely out of my depth when looking at the pianos and I suspected that John was too, but we bluffed our way through looking at and discussing several different ones. Neither of us could really play and I barely remembered what Granny Ward had taught me, but we absorbed as much as we could from the young man before telling him we would come back another day and making our escape out of the shop.

"Did you see the prices!?" I exclaimed under my breath.

He nodded, "We could go to Gent's in Newton Heath," John whispered to me. "They have a fine display there, and they sell gramophones too."

"We can go tomorrow," I suggested as we headed back along Deansgate and Market Street towards the tram and home to South View and a warm fire.

They say that time races by when you're enjoying yourself, and very soon our time together was spent. Just eight days after we were married, John had to go back to camp. I saw him off on the train just like last time; but with more love for him than I had ever felt before in my whole life. He wiped away my tears and laid kisses upon my nose and wet cheeks.

This time he could hold me and kiss me on the platform, as now I was his wife and not just his sweetheart, but that couldn't console me, nor make the time on the cold station platform stand still any longer. The shrill train whistle blew, many carriage doors slammed, and the train slowly pulled away from me, leaving me alone; waving until my love disappeared into the billowing steam that engulfed the train until it was gone.

John wrote often and sent many postcards to me, his loving wife and I replied to him, my dearest husband. My name looked strangely odd when letters arrived; Mrs J.J. Hankinson.

Joe and Ma had taken to using my full-married title for a lark. "Tea's ready Mrs Hankinson," Joe would say in a tease to try to make me smile.

"Post for you Mrs Hankinson," smiled Ma too; I think she understood, but for quite a while I felt forlorn, lost and quite at odds with myself.

A month later a Christmas card came from John. Well, in fact, two cards. One from the Manchester Regiment, issued to each soldier; and another, a much more personal one along with a long letter telling me how much he missed my tender kisses, my laughter and my smile. He was still in Tetney, Leicestershire at a training camp but was hoping to go to France sometime in the New Year, eager to help in the push against the Hun.

He couldn't discuss anything else regarding where he was or any other military matters and so he filled his letters with tiny endearments and frivolous paradiddles.

My letters to him were probably more upbeat than I really felt, and I told him about the quiet Christmas we had spent at home without him and the same flatteries that lovers send to each other when forced apart. My life became a low, slow rhythm of work and sleep, peppered with the occasional elated feeling when I recognised his hand on the envelope.

Lizzie hadn't been well over Christmas and into the New Year. She was anaemic and the doctor recommended some fresh air and good food. Aunt Emily had written to ask Lizzie if she would like to go and spend some time in the countryside with her, the family and cousin Harry of course. He was eight now and doing very well in school, she had written, but one of the other children, Tommy Jones was being mean to him, and she invited Lizzie to stay for a while. Aunt Emily sounded upset in her letter and so Lizzie and I decided to take the train to see the family together.

"Three hours is a long time to sit on a train, Lizzie," I said when it finally arrived at the platform, and we could climb aboard. "Have you brought a book to read?"

"It's alright," she answered. "I will probably sleep all the way there. I'm so tired Beatrice."

I handed my bag up to her and followed her into the carriage. She was opening the compartment doors. There was a man in the first cubicle smoking a pipe and reading a newspaper.

"No," she said, quickly closing the door again.

A family of five in the next compartment too, so that wasn't suitable either. We continued along the passageway until we found an empty one and she drew down the blinds so that it signalled that we weren't to be disturbed.

My heart skipped a beat as I heard the train whistle signal blow, and we slowly eased away from Manchester, to take the journey southwards towards Chirk, Aunt Emily and Cousin Harry.

Chirk is a very nice village and the cottage in Chirk Bank delightful. Little Harry had grown well and was a stout little chap and he ran to hug us both when we arrived. Aunt Emily had made a rabbit stew just like she did in the old days before she moved away, and the kitchen smelled warm and inviting.

"Goodness how you've grown Harry," I said as I removed the large hatpin from my hat. "I swear you get bigger by the day. I only saw you last year and you've shot up!"

"I'm eight now," he said, proudly puffing up his chest, trying to be bigger than he was. Will you come to see my toy trains, Beatrice? We can go for a walk tomorrow too and I'll show you the real trains, they run right by here and sometimes the drivers blow their whistles when I wave. There's a viaduct and an aqueduct too. The trains and the canal go over, and the river goes under," he explained non-stop in his excitement.

I laughed at his childish enthusiasm and told him we had just arrived on the train, and we chattered about the things we had seen on our journey. He was eager to show us around his village. The last time we had been there was when he was only small and he didn't remember, even though they had visited Failsworth several times in between then and now.

While Lizzie unpacked and chatted to Aunt Emily, I allowed Cousin Harry to show me around the cottage. It was larger than it looked from the outside and was set back off the main street, surrounded by pretty fields.

"This is my bedroom," he announced when we had climbed up the very steep stairs to the attic room. His toy train was on a small table in front of the little dormer window. On top of his chest of drawers at the other side of the little room was a magic lantern, another of his prized possessions. He lit the candle and showed me the glass slides that had pictures of the Boer war on and the battles that the British army, helped by the Dublin

Fusiliers had fought in Elandslaagte, Modder River and Pieters Hill; and the attack the Boers made on the armoured train at Chieveley near Ladysmith, where the Boers took prisoners to Pretoria.

"Goodness Harry, you're very knowledgeable," I said as he told me all about the battles.

"Soldiers are very brave men," he announced as he carefully packed the slides away again in their little drawer within the case. "You should be very proud of your husband."

I raised my eyebrows at him and his maturity for an eight-year-old and smiled my thank you to him, turning to look out of the window once more.

"It's a lovely view Harry," I said. "We're very high up."

"Look, a train!" He pointed over to the left, where we could see the steam as the train puffed its way through the countryside.

The garden below us was neat and well organised, the new spring growth starting to show through the dark, delicious soil in the afternoon sunshine.

"Do you help your Ma in the garden Harry?" I asked.

"Yes," he scowled. "But only when William isn't around, he pushes me over and I fall into the flower beds. Then mother gets cross with him, and it makes it all worse."

Don't miss the last train home

"Poor you," I answered, putting a protective arm around my young cousin's shoulder. "I'll have a word with that boy," I promised as we made our way back downstairs for tea.

Yet again, time flew for Lizzie and me. Very soon our lovely week came to an end, and we said our goodbyes and left promises that we would go over to visit again as soon as we could.

Our train happily chugged its way through the beautiful countryside where trees and green fields and farms ticked pleasantly by in the afternoon sunshine until we approached the city, where the smog obscured the sun, and the gloomy factories and dark mill buildings became the only view. The train slowly pulled into Manchester Piccadilly station, and we were home once more.

Home and back to a new calamity. Ma was out but Joe was sitting in the rocking chair, his left arm in a sling.

"What ho you two!" he called as we came into the room, taking off our hats and chattering loudly about our trip.

"Joe! What on earth have you done now?" exclaimed Lizzie as she saw him. "Your arm?"

"I hurt it at work," he said casually, laughing at our shocked faces.

"Just how?" we both asked together.

"I was in the weaving shed yesterday and one of the pulleys caught my shirt," he explained as Lizzie walked over to him to inspect his arm. He pulled away. "It doesn't hurt now… but it did. It pulled my shirtsleeve and took me up with it. Then it flipped me right over and I landed on the floor! It's not broken, it's just twisted and bruised." He laughed with false bravado.

I shook my head in astonishment as he showed us both the bruising on his upper arm. His shoulder was black and blue and there was a large gash on his arm, a scar of congealed blood clotting on his skin.

"Goodness me, you're lucky you weren't more seriously hurt!" I said, remembering all too acutely the accident that Eunice had only three years ago.

Lizzie sat down at the table looking quite shocked. The trip to Aunt Emily's had done her good but she looked pale again now we were home, quite probably because of the shock of seeing Joe injured and reminding her too of our little sister.

"You'd better be more careful, Joe," she said with a sigh, shaking her head at him as she sat down at the table, "I can't take any more. Put the kettle on Beatie please love."

I stepped over the bags we had dumped on the floor as we came in and reached over to get the kettle off the hearth.

Don't miss the last train home

"Another letter came for you Mrs Hankinson," he said, getting up and going over to the dresser. He handed it to me, and I recognised my dear Johns handwriting on it. I carefully put it in my pocket to read when I was alone later.

I finally managed to get upstairs shortly after tea and after we had told Ma all about our visit to Aunt Emily's. I sat down on the edge of the bed to read my letter and to look at the postcard he had sent to me. It was a silk one again and it held the words, 'Love me and the world is mine' embroidered on it.

His letter was full of love and sweetness, as usual, making me yearn and long for his touch once more. He felt so very far away.

Time passed and the following month would be my John's twenty first birthday. I had already written to tell him about our trip to Chirk and Joe's accident and I now sat at the kitchen table to write out the words on the embroidered silk birthday card I had found for him.

> *My dear Husband,*
> *I am so very sorry you are not at home this time as you were last time so good luck and best love.*
> *From your ever loving wife Beatrice.*

I carefully drew the symbol for infinity as I always do and spelled out LOVE in little kisses.

"Tell him my arm is a little better," Joe said, looking over my shoulder as I wrote, and so I added those words too.

Joe a little better.

Then I popped it in the envelope and headed out to catch the afternoon post.

I was so very lonely. Not for company, I had plenty of that, but I thought how sad it was that he could not be home with me. I had wondered since being a little girl, what it would be like when I would fall in love and marry a handsome man. I grew up waiting for love to happen and now that I have it, a war in a foreign land had taken him away from me. I missed him so terribly and I don't suppose I would ever be happy until he came home to me again. All I had were his cards and letters and I carefully kept them all in my box, under my bed.

Not too long after my own twenty first birthday that year, he wrote to tell me that he was to be posted to the western front. Ypres in Belgium was all he could tell me, he had said. Later that year the Manchester Regiment was to be disbanded and he was now assigned to the 11th Border Regiment. He had a new number, 28773 and all my letters would be redirected to him at the front. I think that was when I realised the real danger my dearest John was in. I pleaded with him to stay safe and to come home to me.

Don't miss the last train home

I waited that whole year for his letters; each time one arrived I scurried away so that I could read them in private. I have no desire to share his words, his loving tenderness to me, with anyone.

I read letters from the brave soldier, about the camaraderie of the boys in his company and a little of the fighting and the conditions. The words he used were brave and courageous. He told of the fun he was having. He sent photographs of groups of lads in their barracks and camps; all smiling, all jovial and carefree.

Reading in between the lines of his letters though, I heard the homesick man, the young lover who needed his wife as much as she did him. His letters grew shorter. He had seen death now, the death of some of his friends. At first his letters had portrayed a great adventure, but now the dirt and mud, the noise of the guns and the constant shelling were taking their toll on him. The marching from one place to another to reinforce the front lines didn't sound like fun anymore and I also heard from the newsstands and gossip in the street, just how many of our young soldiers were being killed in the field.

Christmas that year was accompanied by a Border Regiment Christmas card and another, a much more personal one; and a most beautiful letter that I shall keep with me forevermore. His words were much more tender, much more haunting and I longed for him to come home and hold me in his arms once more.

Chapter nineteen

March 1918 and

beyond

I was numb. Not with fear but with an unfolding realisation of the senselessness of it all and a growing awareness of the danger my John was in. Allied losses were growing in the tens of thousands, all for a few yards of ground... and the months ticked by.

I suppose now looking back, I should have been more fearful but in March a letter arrived for me, and I immediately knew what it would say. I froze to the spot as I saw Lizzie take it from the messenger in the courtyard. She slowly turned to hand it to me, and I saw her eyes widen as she looked at me, a chill filled the silence, and everything went black.

I looked up from the floor where I had collapsed. Joe was straightening my legs and Ma knelt by my side, patting my face, she had tears in her eyes. I looked over to my left to see Lizzie sitting on the floor tiles in the doorway where she had slid down the wall, tears streaming down her face too, the front door wide open in the spring sunshine.

We all knew what would be in the unopened letter that Lizzie still held in her hand. We all knew in that instant that my John would never come home to me.

That moment, there in the doorway, all my hopes and dreams drained from me. No emotion, no feeling and no tears; just a hollowness inside me that didn't even hurt.

"Can you stand Beatrice?" Ma asked. "Come on love, let's get you up."

She and Joe helped me to stand, and I floated over to the rocking chair where I started to rock, forwards and backwards in time with the ticking of the clock. After a short while, Lizzie's hand trembled as she offered the letter to me and I mechanically opened the envelope, unfolding and reading the words in a completely different hand than the familiar one I wanted to see.

The words told me how John was a good soldier, well-liked by his comrades and that he had unfortunately been killed in action on the 3rd of March. He was in the front-line trenches, and a mortar shell had exploded close by him.

The letter fell to the floor.

I had taken a few days to quietly absorb the fact that I was a widow at the age of twenty-one and I still hadn't shed a tear. Neither had his mother when I called to tell them the tragic news.

"Mary, pop the kettle on, our Beatrice is here," John's dad shouted to his wife as he opened the door to me. "Come in, love…" he stopped speaking as he looked at my face.

"Here, sit down," he pulled a chair from under the table and guided me to it.

Mary Ellen turned from the range where she had just poured more water into the kettle on the fire and a contorted look spread across her face as she looked at me.

"No!" she said, already guessing why I was there and what news I had come to impart to them.

"No!" she said again, and grabbed the edge of her apron, drying her hands to take the letter I held in my outstretched hand from me.

John turned away and placed one hand on the mantle above the fire, his head slumped forwards to rest on his hand. Mary Ellen opened the letter with trembling hands.

"My boy," she whispered. "My poor boy."

She slowly folded the letter and slid it back into the envelope, placing it between us on the table.

"I'm sorry," I offered meekly, knowing that those words were not enough but they hung in the air long after they were said.

"Proud of him I am!" John finally turned to face us both, slamming his fist into the palm of his hand. "Proud of my boy… He fought for King and country! They can't take that away from us, Mary. Proud that he played his part." He turned back to face the mantlepiece, his shoulders rigid, his back straight. "Proud… yes proud!"

The rest of his family were as quiet as I was; stunned, I think. Lily and Elizabeth, both hugged me tightly without speaking and I walked away from their house leaving them as bereft and as lost as I was. There was nothing more to say.

"Whatever shall I do Lizzie?" I asked.
She and I were sat in the courtyard, she on an upturned wooden crate and myself on a large rockery stone. The weather was warm with the promise of a nice Easter, but I was cold inside. She didn't know how to answer me and so we sat there together in silence looking at a patch of daffodils

by the door waiting to burst from their buds and proclaim their joy.

"We should pick some and put them in a vase for Ma, they will open sooner inside," she said, and I nodded my silent agreement.

"I'm sorry Bea, I don't know what to say. I suppose we just must carry on, like all the other times. Ma always said, we must keep strong – life goes on."

"I expect it does," I replied, looking over at her although, I wasn't sure I agreed with her. "Have you heard from Alex?"

"Occasionally yes, but he and I didn't really part as friends."

"I'm sorry," I whispered. "Not working out well for us, is it?"

She looked at me and wiped away a tear from her cheek. "We will survive. We will find love again," she determined. She was always more optimistic than I was. I doubted I would ever feel anything, ever again. My soul was dry, my heart empty and I simply had to continue to go through the motions of everyday life, just like I had for the last year and a half since our wedding... since he went away.

Then I had hope that he would come back to me; now... I knew he wouldn't.

Joe came through the alley in front of us carrying a large heavy flat box. He placed it down on the old rickety potting table that stood underneath the window, and took off his cap, wiping his brow with his shirt sleeve.

"Good morning sisters." he smiled and swooped a bow in jest. "I bet you can't guess what I've bought?"

I looked over to look at the box. I could see the name of the shop printed on it. Gents, 704 Oldham Road, Newton Heath where John and I had bought the gramophone. It sat un-played and gathering dust in the front room along with his piano, waiting for his return too.

"Looks heavy," replied Lizzie. "What have you bought now Joe?"

"A zither," he announced to our curious and puzzled faces.

"A what?"

"A zither," he proudly said again. "My very own zither."

I saw a confused frown tickle Lizzies face and I watched as she stood up to see Joe open the box and lift out a wooden board with metal strings attached to it rather like a harp. He sat down on the box where Lizzie had been sitting opposite me and placed the zither flat on his knee with the narrow end at a slight angle facing me. Then with a small pick held between his finger and thumb of his right hand, he strummed across the strings. Then he started to pluck each string on the right-hand side of it. They were sweet and shrill. With the pick on his left forefinger, he gently strummed the thicker strings; the mellow chords and he gently damped them with the pad of his left thumb.

"It's a beautiful sound, Joe!" I gasped. "I've never seen or heard anything like it."

"Do you know any tunes?" asked Lizzie.

"I know lots of tunes," he boasted. Then he laughed when he admitted he would have to practice before he could play any.

Joe and I spent the next few days in our front room; I seated at John's piano gently caressing the keys until I found the courage to make a note; and he sat cross-legged on the floor, his zither on his knee, gently strumming the strings in a blind attempt to make it sound like a tune we might recognise.

"I remember that this is middle C," I said, hitting the key with my middle finger, Granny Wards teachings filtering through the mist of time in my head.

Joe replied by plucking the string that sounded the most same and that is where we started from. "C, it's here on this sheet music, this is it," he plucked the strings, and we played the notes together.

Eventually between us, we worked out what notes sounded the same and with the help of the notation that was printed in gold on the soundboard of the zither, we learned together which notes were the ones that sounded good together and made a tune.

All the little melodies, jingles and things that Granny Ward had taught me came back from where they had lain hidden by the pain of the loss of her. Our days that summer were filled with notes of music that gradually filled the emptiness of this new grief as I struggled to heal my heart once more. Joe and I spent day after day picking out the notes and learning how to make harmonious music that we could be proud of.

That was the thing with Joe; he always found entertaining ways to make us all happy, his jovial disposition would cheer the darkest day, he was so gentle; a pleasure to talk to. He often came home with something nice that helped me fritter away the hours of that wet and dull summer, a bag of sweets or a new little poem that we would try to make a tune to. I don't think I realised at the time, just how much Joe helped me and maybe I looked to him for motivation. With every loss of someone that I had loved, I had withdrawn inside myself, not wanting to allow my feelings get the better of me and promising myself that I wouldn't ever love again. But Joe understood somehow and drew that out of me. He didn't know it, but he helped me to give myself permission to play John's piano. That was indeed a huge hurdle.

I enjoyed being with Joe and Lizzie too, although she was much less sensitive than I was; she always looked on the bright side of everything as if it was normal to move on.

One Saturday, Joe had been at work to earn some overtime; one of the looms had jammed, something had broken, and he had offered to help to fix it, earning him an extra sixpence for his trouble. Lizzie had gone to Tommyfield market in Oldham with Elsie Haslem in search of ribbons and sweets; and Ma was busying herself at the allotment, which meant tomatoes, lettuce, cheese and homemade pickle for tea with strawberries to follow; and so, I was alone with my thoughts and my piano.

My piano?

Was I healing?

I started to sing as I played.

> *"On a hill far away stood an old rugged cross,*
> *The emblem of suffering and shame.*
> *And I love that old cross where the dearest and best,*
> *For a world of lost sinners was slain.*
> *So, I'll cherish the old rugged cross..., rugged cross,*

Till my trophies at last I lay down,
I will cling to the old rugged cross,
And exchange it some day for a crown."

It was a tune I had always liked from school, and we had chosen it at our wedding. Singing with the confidence of being alone I staged a performance to myself although I knew I was singing quite loudly in my high-pitched voice. Such a shame that Eunice wasn't here; her voice would have been far nicer. I blinked those thoughts away as I didn't want to cry... not again. I must remain strong... stoic, and as much as it might hurt, it was over, and I had to move forward and singing loudly helped.

Joe burst in just then, mid hymn and broke my imagined harmony.

He was laughing.

"Goodness Beatie!" he jeered, "I could hear that racket above the noise of the mill!"

"Very drôle," I sniffed, glad for the distraction. "Is the loom mended?"

"Yes, Mr Benson was very pleased and gave me an extra tuppence."

He dropped his jacket on the floor and sat cross-legged on the rug, taking up his zither onto his knee. He started to strum it to check it was in tune.

"Joe!" I said as I looked at his heap of a jacket. "Your coat is moving!"

"Oh yes, I forgot. I found this near the canal." He dove into his pocket and pulled out a black and white fluffy ball, reaching out to place it in my outstretched hands.

"A puppy!" I squealed. "Oh, what a sweet little thing." I held the little fluff ball up to look at his face and a pink tongue started to lick my wrist.

"Meet Laddie," Joe started to plink out a new tune to welcome the pocket-sized puppy into our home as I sat and cuddled Laddie, fondling his soft little ears and feeling a lot better than I had for a long while.

I took it upon myself to take him outside every half an hour until he was toilet trained; and I would collect the scraps from our plates for his tea. When there were no scraps, he would enjoy bread with an oxo sprinkled over it. In return, he would follow me around and often came to greet me at the mill gates when work was over for the day.

Tinker joined our family that year too; she was a Persian tabby kitten, her fluffy tail longer than most cats' tails. Ma said she could stay because she dusted as she balanced carefully on the furniture, tippytoeing around on her dainty little paws. She earned her name by the way she delicately walked over the keys of my piano. I wondered if she knew her scales, for she never played a wrong note.

"Tinkerbell, the kitten on the keys," Joe named her, and there was a little poem written too. She had followed Joe home about six weeks after Laddie had arrived and the pair became great friends, curling up together to sleep when they had finished playing.

Then the Armistice came.

The eleventh hour, of the eleventh day, of the eleventh month. The Church bells that could not ring their joy for my wedding to John, rang out loud and clear for the end of the Great War.

That was when the tears came. When the great lump in my throat became a sob and the warm prickles behind my eyes finally spilt over and ran down my cheeks. My shaking hands held a flag and my aching arms waved; my empty voice cheered as processions of tired and wounded soldiers came triumphant home to Failsworth.

But the dark grief inside me would not fade with the memories of the war and the fact that John was not among them. I lied when I said I was glad it was over as that was too final. Every day when I woke, I could, for that brief waking moment feel him with me, but the thought that he might return faded with the dawn into the knowledge that he never would.

I didn't know how I would ever move on - but I did, little by little with the help of Laddie and Tinker. I didn't have any choice. I had to work every day and eat and sleep. I wasn't happy with my work in the mill, but I didn't know what I might do instead and the thought of going to Manchester to work unnerved me a lot.

That was until a chance meeting with and friend of Ma's called Mrs Mary Faulkener, a widow with two married daughters older than we were. She was a milliner and seamstress working from home above a little shop on Oldham Road. I had noted that it was being renovated the last time I passed by.

I came home from work one evening to see her sitting in our kitchen with Ma, drinking tea.

"Good evening, Ma," I said, "Hello Mrs Faulkener," nodding my head politely to her as I took off my shawl on entering the room. I sat down and took the cup of freshly poured tea from Ma's hand.

"Hello Beatrice," she answered kindly. "How are you love?"

"Managing," I smiled, feeling every ounce that I wasn't. "Are you well?

"It isn't easy is it?" answering with a question to hide her embarrassment, she blinked hard and shifted her position on the hard-backed chair.

"Now listen Beatrice, I met your Ma earlier and I was telling her how I am looking for a shop-girl to help me in my shop if you're interested?"

I could feel the excitement rise. Everyone knew how I loved hats and fashion. Eunice and I had collected photographic cards with Mary Pickford, Dorothy Minto and other photographic models on them. Gladys Cooper, the actress being our favourite. We tried to style our hair like them, collected feathers and bought scraps of felt to try to copy their hat fashions. We practised their poses in front of our bedroom mirror, collapsing in fits of giggles... before she fell ill.

Before she died.

Some of those cards were in my box upstairs. A shudder ran through me, and I closed my eyes and mind to the memories.

I looked at Ma, whose expression didn't change as she sipped her hot tea. I smiled a touch as I then realised, she had known how sad I had been and that she had discussed all this before today with Mrs Faulkener.

Hmmm, that's why she was in our kitchen, and it also explained the freshly baked biscuits on the plate between them.

I took a while to answer and tried to sound more cautious and restrained than I felt.

"A shop girl?" I smiled, pretending to ponder the opportunity. The younger Beatrice would have jumped in and said *"yes! ooooh yes please!"* but I was much more guarded these days. Safe to say that if I had been more aware of the chance of becoming a young widow so soon, I would never have allowed myself to fall head over heels in love with a soldier, and I most certainly would never have married him in wartime.

I took a cautious sip of my tea swallowing the hot liquid before I looked up again at her.

"I... I don't think so Mrs Faulkener, thank you all the same,"

Both women looked astonished at me and then at each other. I couldn't explain why; not with words, but my heart was empty of the passion I once felt. There was an awkward silence between us as we sipped our tea.

"Are you sure you won't think about it Beatrice dear? I think you would like what I have in mind for the shop and what I could do with is the help," she pushed, and I made the mistake of looking her straight in the eyes. I couldn't speak but a lonely tear escaped and ran down my cheek.

Ma looked at me, her eyes were full of concern and worry as Lizzie bounced into the room and broke the spell by asking what was being discussed. As Ma started to explain, I could see by the look on Lizzie's excited face that she thought I should at least give the job a chance.

"I'm surprised at you Beatrice, what a great opportunity. You love hats and fashion!" she enthused, seeing my frightened and timid face.

I nodded slowly and agreed that my head did indeed reason that I should at least give it a try, as uneasy and nervous as I was.

A fortnight later I tentatively walked down Oldham Road to go and meet Mrs Faulkener at the shop at number 278. The smell of fresh paint greeted me as I cautiously opened the door; the little bell tinkled my entrance. I stood, looking around the shop to take in my new surroundings. The sight was a whole world away from the noise and bustle of the mill and yet I don't know what I had expected. I had been in the haberdashery stores in Manchester many times and they had been full of fabrics and ribbons and bows. Our favourite shops had always been Lewis' and Affleck & Browns on Market Street. But they were large, well-established companies and this was just a little shop in Failsworth.

The floor was bare and there was a lad, younger than Joe, on his knees, scrubbing the boards with a large, bristled brush and hot soapy water. He didn't stop or look up as I entered the shop, and I stood awkwardly with my hand on the door handle.

There was an empty haberdasher's glass topped counter with empty drawers in it to my left and another glass fronted display case next to the whitewashed brick wall. On my right, in front of the window was a table with one or two empty hat blocks upon it and a tall contraption made of wood and wire, which had the familiar look of a mannequin. Four or five cardboard boxes were stacked next to two upholstered chairs with a rolled-up rug leant against them. Then some shelving with just a few rolls of cloth placed on them in no particular order.

"There you are Beatrice," Mrs Faulkener's voice from the back of the shop broke my reverie and she came towards me carrying another large box, which she placed on the glass-topped counter.

"Take off your coat dear and pop it downstairs," she ordered. "Then come and help me to unpack these new ribbons. I would like you to fill those empty drawers with them over here." She nodded where she wanted me to put them in the empty drawers I had seen earlier.

"Sam, when you've finished and the floor is dry, can you take these chairs and the rug to the back of the shop. Don't put the rug on the floor until it's dry." The boy nodded and carried on scrubbing as I stepped over his pail and walked through to the back of the shop. A flight of stairs

247

rose to my right and light was coming from a small window on the landing. In front of me was another flight of stone steps going down. I descended into a poorly lit cellar that had also been freshly whitewashed. There was a large, bolted back door, and a scrubbed pine table in the centre of the room. A stone sink was in the corner and a bentwood coat stand to the side, where I hurriedly hung my coat before climbing back up into the shop.

Mrs Faulkener had taken some of the ribbons out of the box and she showed me how she wanted me to arrange them in colour order in the display cupboard.

"Such a shortage after the war, this is all I could get," she explained, perhaps more to herself than to me. "I hope there will be another delivery before we sell out." She left me to do the task and busied herself with another box that contained cards of buttons, which she placed in a couple of the drawers in the glass-topped counter.

The ribbons were soft and silky in my fingers and the colours were bright and gay. I quickly sorted them into a rainbow of colours, separating the shades and different widths and placing them neatly side-by-side in the cabinet. As I finished the ribbons, she lifted another box onto the counter and turned to smile at me. That smile captured both her excitement and my own as together we filled as best we could the drawers and display case with the items she had managed to buy from her wholesalers.

Later that afternoon a carrier arrived with the fabrics that she had ordered. The boy, Sam and I helped to bring them into the shop where we placed them on the shelving. The floor was now dry, and Sam had placed the rug on the floor and the chairs were arranged for customers to sit on.

I took a final look behind me as I left at five o'clock to go home, excited for the first time in a long time at the prospect of a new day tomorrow and hoping that Mrs Faulkener was pleased with what I had done.

Karol Darnell

Chapter twenty

Hats

It was one of those motionless icy mornings where the cold air is still and mist hangs in the air like the vapour from a steam kettle. A tranquil morning, where it is usually difficult to get out of the relative warmth of bed to face the long cold walk to work, yet it is serene in beauty and stillness. The cogs of life start to turn, and the noise of the mills crank up their mechanical music. Silent iciness dusts the pavements, each leaf and frond sprinkled with a sugar coating of frost; the twigs and sticks bare in the front courtyard as I look out through the crystal swirls of ice that decorate the inside of the windowpane. The dark silhouettes of mill chimneys and rooftops shrouded in the thick mist and the pea soup fog hides the usually familiar trees along the canal towpath as I glance to my right before making my way along Wrigley Head to the corner where it meets Oldham Road, past the Pole, over the busy canal again near the wharf and on down towards the shop.

My breath steams from my mouth and leaves a drip on the end of my nose as I walk along, stepping carefully around the frozen glassy puddles; more eager than I have ever been to get to work. I consider for a moment how wretched I used to feel, trudging along at first light to the mill. My life now is easier. I start work at eight in the morning, a full two hours later than before, and I smile to myself inside the scarf I have wrapped around my face against the cold air.

The familiar little shop bell tinkles as I enter the shop to see a lady standing there waiting for me.

"Good morning," we both say in unison, smiling at each other.

"May I help you?" I add, unwrapping myself from my scarf and taking off my gloves.

"I'm here to see Mrs Faulkener," she explained. "Annie Clarke, for the position of assistant seamstress. I saw the advertisement in the Oldham Chronicle." She handed the torn-off piece of newspaper to me.

"Ah, of course. Please come with me." I smiled at her as I led her upstairs to where Mary Faulkener had her workrooms.

News of the quality of Mrs Faulkener's dresses and the success of our little shop had spread by word of mouth, and new customers started to make the journey from Manchester and beyond. She made dresses and hats for some very fine ladies indeed. We had been so busy these past few weeks that she hadn't been able to keep up with demand and she had so many orders for dresses to be made that she had placed an advertisement for an assistant seamstress.

Annie Clarke seemed to fit the bill completely. She had experience in dressmaking and, although she was older than me, we got on very well.

Every morning, Mrs Faulkener would explain what our jobs were for the day and what orders we each had. Annie would mostly help Mrs Faulkener upstairs with the dressmaking but was to help in the shop if we were busy. For the most part, however, this was my domain. I was to greet and serve the customers who came into the shop; some would just want a new set of buttons; others came to browse for new fabrics or lace and ribbons. Our reputation continued to grow as chic and stylish dressmakers, and I became more knowledgeable about the styles and fashions in this post-war period of change.

"There is a small box of pieces of fabric and ribbons here Beatrice," Mrs Faulkener announced a few weeks later. She placed a small brown box on the counter in front of me; it had a brown ribbon around it and a bow on the top, holding the lid on. I carefully untied the bow to open the little treasure trove of fabric pieces and I excitedly looked through them.

"I thought I might order some hat bases for you to practice on. I want you to try to trim them up. You're a young lady and you seem to know about what fashion the young folk might like these days. Then I will teach you how to make a hat from the beginning when you've got the hang of it." she said.

"That's a thrilling idea," I replied, my mind already racing as I sorted through the pieces of tulle, velvets, ribbon and grosgrain with my eager fingers.

"See what ideas come into your head and I will write an order to Failsworth Hats to buy some hat bases."

With that, she left me to look through the contents of the box. A green and white striped piece of grosgrain caught my eye.

It was about thirty inches long and just enough to go around the crown of a straw boater, replacing the dark brown ribbon that did the hat no justice whatsoever. I carefully stitched the ends of the ribbon together and placed the boater on a hat block on the counter, standing back to admire my first creation. A thinner piece of red checked ribbon, I placed to one side, as I knew this piece of ribbon would likely be used similarly when I found another boater to use it on.

Next, I found six small squares of printed cotton in various colours and, running a stitch around the perimeter, I gathered one of the little pieces of fabric up into a ball and stitched a small bead into the centre, pulling the midpoint inwards. I had created a flower. Deftly working the same magic with the other pieces, soon I had half a dozen flowers that I could already envisage decorating a wide-brimmed ladies' hat with. In my mind I could see that imagined hat already poised on the head of a lady whilst walking upon a seaside promenade.

Chuckling to myself, I delved deeper into the little box. A pale blue piece of crushed velvet, a smaller black bit and a beautiful long piece of blue slub silk also made me ponder; but these would have to wait until the hat bases arrived. Two pieces of lilac chiffon floated as I caressed it through my fingers and my imaginative mind while I anticipated the day that I could give flight to my ideas.

I could hardly sleep that night as the colourful fabrics, hats, felt, and feathers drifted through my head.

By the end of the week, though, I had been given free creative rein on hat designs and decoration. Mrs Faulkener showed me how to stitch the decorations onto the hats properly and I quickly learned what worked and what didn't. I scoured the lady's magazines with what designs were new in London and Paris, replicating many whilst giving other ideas a novel twist. All reordering and dealing with shop matters fell onto my shoulders, and I grew in confidence as the weeks ticked by.

A fashionable dress now hung on the mannequin. Annie and I had found a picture in a French fashion magazine, and we coerced Mrs Faulkener to make it; the skirt was shorter in length as it was now stylish to show just above the ankle. It had a striped blouse and a lower collar at the neckline. To compliment this outfit, I had designed a smaller hat with a less flouncy brim, three neat striped flowers in the same fabric as the blouse, adorned the side. Now from outside the window, we enticed shoppers into coming in to view what was for sale inside. I had placed three hat blocks on another counter next to the window to the right and we were now displaying three of the most elaborate and decorative hat creations ever seen; plumes of huge ostrich feathers and a sage green silk bow adorned one made from a dark green tartan. Next to that, a red hat with a narrow brim and trimmed with pretty lace and the flowers that I had made.

The last hat was a more sombre affair in black, with the piece of black velvet as a trim and a veil of dark lace; too elaborate to be for a funeral but was obviously a more fashionable driving or riding hat. Someone from Cheshire might fancy themselves in that. So, we provided for all tastes and ages, from smart young ladies to our reliable and dependable older clientele.

Lady's embroidered gloves and feathered fascinators, folding fans, hatpins, combs and other fashionable trinkets were now displayed inside the shop and woollen hat felt was neatly stacked in colour order on a shelf behind the counter. Trilby's, gentlemen's woollen caps and leather driving gloves were displayed on another cabinet. We still had many spaces to be filled as supplies were slow to arrive, but I made the most of the display space and I hoped any gaps weren't too obvious.

"I'm going to Doncaster next week," announced Annie one afternoon as she swept the floor of the shop before we closed. "The Mrs is letting me have a few days off." The weather was getting warmer as summer approached and we had been discussing holidays.

Many of our customers were talking about going to the seaside again this year but our family had never had much money for outings any further than our local haunts. There were a few postcards in my box from before the war that were sent by friends.

Mrs Ashton had sent one from Blackpool only last year too.

I also treasured the ones that Elsie had sent Eunice, but holidays weren't ever considered in our family before now. My mind was on my postcards, and I hadn't been listening to Annie.

"Have you ever been to the races Beatrice?"

"No...Er...no, I've only ever been to Oswestry, Chirk actually, to visit my Aunt Emily a couple of years ago...and..." I gathered up the felt flowers that I had made and placed them in a drawer to distract myself from my thoughts of John and the day I took a trip to Altcar to visit him before we were married and the impact of his proposal and what it had meant to me.

"Albert has a cousin who lives there, and we've been invited to stay with him." she continued.

"That sounds nice, will you send me a postcard?"

"Of course I will," she laughed as the shop bell tinkled once more.

Joe and a couple of his friends stood in the doorway.

"Good afternoon, Joe, what do you want?" I was suspicious of the reason for his visit to the shop.

"We thought we would walk you home Miss," replied one of the other lads.

"Thank you, Eric," I replied stiffly. "I think I know the way."

"It's a nice evening." offered Enoch, one of Joe's newest friends.

I looked at their eager faces and then at Joe. "I'll get my hat," I replied, secretly scowling at his bright and not so innocent face. *I'll get to you later*!

The walk home was as awkward as I had anticipated. Both boys were very nice, but I had guessed their motives correctly.

It seemed that in their silly flush of youthfulness, they thought that they could attempt to court me. As if it were a game to see who might steal the attention of a young widow. They each tried in their own immature way to interest me in walking out with them.

I was more than a little irritated and yet a touch flattered, although I managed to keep that feeling very well hidden when I pounced on Joe when we got home.

"Owww!" he yelled as I threw a cushion off the rocking chair at him. He started to laugh, and I regained possession of the cushion, hitting him round the head with it in playful jest.

259

"Don't... you... ever!" I shouted, trying so very hard to stem my fit of giggles at my rage and his mischievous face.

"You'd like Ted though," He shouted as he ducked and darted for the door. "Teddy is great fun."

I growled at him ready to throw the cushion at him again; but quickly placed it back on the rocking chair as I saw Ma come in from the allotment carrying a bowl of freshly picked peas ready to be podded for tea. There was nothing like the approach of a mother to instantly quell a childish dispute.

"What are you laughing at?" she quizzed. I think she had seen me with the cushion in my hands.

"Just at how silly my brother is," I answered with a grin, and quickly changed the subject as I followed her into the kitchen to help her pod the peas into a large pan.

"You're so much prettier when you smile, Beatrice."

Annie was true to her word, and she did remember to send me a postcard from Doncaster. On the back, she wrote:

> *Dear friend, Having lovely weather, very hot. Do wish you were here we would have such fun. I am*

*going to the races tomorrow there are a lot of
people. Best love from your friend, A Clarke.*

I decided that I would send one back to her as
she had given me the address of her brother-in-law
in Doncaster. I wished that she would be careful
and to only bet on the horse that was sure to win
and the day after another one arrived from her
again.

*Dear Friend, Received PC thanks very much.
Had a good time at the races. You might hope
the people that are here shall be coming back
fortuitous (worst luck) Then it's work. The Mrs
has wrote to me. Keep smiling all for all when
home free. Annie*

I laughed at what she had written on her card.

"Oh Annie!" I said out loud, 'The Mrs!' Ha,
she calls her 'the Mrs'.

I placed the card above the fireplace chuckling
to myself and thought no more of it as I walked to
work.

By the end of that year and a few postcards later
from both Eric and Enoch too, I was feeling much
more self-confident, and the shop was looking
splendid, modern and very well stocked.

The wooden floorboards had been cleaned
and polished to a deep oak colour and a larger and
much nicer rug lay on the floor at the back of the
shop, where the chairs were placed for customers

to sit upon. A large oval floor mirror was now positioned to the right of the chairs and there was also a small table upon which customers could be served tea. The glass-topped haberdasher's counter with wooden display drawers had been filled with colourful ribbons in different widths, braiding and threads of all shades; we had needles, pins and dainty scissors in some of the other drawers, another held reels of lace, the next stored cords, shoe and bootlaces. Next to that was the glass-fronted display case with trays of buttons of every size and shape. We now had roll upon roll of colourful fabric too, from gentle light-coloured silks and printed cotton to heavy velvets of the darkest blue and forest green, presented for customers on our shelving; and such a constant stream of customers that we now opened on a Saturday too to fit them all in.

Chapter twenty-one

Holidays

Mrs Bentley stood in front of the long mirror at the back of the shop, turning her head this way and that, admiring the new hat that I had just finished making for her. It was a cloche style hat in a kingfisher blue crushed velvet with a subtle bow in a lighter shade of blue, as its only decoration. The brim was smaller than on the hats she had previously worn, and it had a slight gathering to it that caused the velvet to catch the light, giving it depth and movement. She used to wear such elaborate, wide-brimmed hats trimmed with feathers and lace, but I had convinced her to try my latest design on and she looked wonderful in it. She was an elegant lady, younger than she acted, I guessed and was married into a very well-to-do family. Her attitude and demeanour obscured the amiable lady inside that I could see. Annie said she wasn't a pleasant customer, too demanding; but I saw past the outward, brash superiority and could see a woman who, quite probably had never seen any hardships. Tainted by a life of affluence and money, but perhaps that was not her fault any more than the hardships in my life were mine.

"Oh Beatrice," she sighed as she preened herself. "It's so... simply handsome. The loveliest creation and suits me so well, don't you think?"

"I do Mrs Bentley. You look quite fine, and very fashionable. You will be the envy of all your friends." I agreed, congratulating myself on making our prestigious client happy.

"I shall wear it this weekend when we go to Morecambe Bay. Everyone will be there, you know. Simply everyone will love it."

She left the shop in her usual flurry, and I went upstairs to tell Mary; The Mrs, ha! about Mrs Bentley's new hat.

I knocked gently as I entered the workroom to see one of Mary's daughters with her.

"Beatrice, how lovely to see you again," Phoebe Lambert said, stepping forward to shake my hand. "Mother tells me you have made some fine hats and the customers love them."

"Yes, hello Mrs Lambert," I smiled at her. "Mrs Bentley is completely happy with the blue cloche hat I made last week," I said to both her and Mary. "She's taking it on her holidays to the seaside to show off to all her friends."

"Thank you, Beatrice, that's wonderful," Mary said, clapping her hands together and smiling up at me. "Our reputation is growing far and wide, you see, Phoebe."

"I'm so pleased mother, well done Beatrice," Phoebe smiled kindly. "That's what I came to tell you. Mother, Herbert and I are taking little Joyce to New Brighton next week. I'm so in need of a holiday and Joyce will so enjoy making sand pies."

The tinkle of the shop bell interrupted our conversation, and I turned away to go back downstairs to tend to our next customer.

"Excuse me, please. I hope you have fun, Mrs Lambert. Give my love to your little girl." I replied over my shoulder.

Exactly one week later, I glanced at the calendar on the wall as I did most mornings, almost not noticing the date until I looked again.

Thursday, 27th May 1920.

The post-boy had just handed me some letters, mostly for Mrs Faulkener and the shop, but there was one addressed to me from Phoebe Lambert in New Brighton.

"She remembered," smiled Mary, handing the card back to me as she took the other letters. "I told her you collected postcards… Are you all right dear? You look upset."

"Yes… I'm fine. I just forgot John's birthday by nearly three weeks, and I only just realised," I said. "How could I forget?"

"We do, dear. Life moves on. My Edward died and left me with two very small girls, and we got through; had to. Your ma, the same," she said, with an air of acceptance that I had come to understand so very well.

"Perhaps you need a holiday too dear, take some time to see the seaside. I know a very nice lady, Mrs Fish, who runs a guest house in Blackpool."

"Yes, Mrs Ashton stays with her when she goes to Blackpool; perhaps I do need to get away." I agreed as she disappeared upstairs once more.

Two whole years had passed, and that numb ache had gone. It was true; I had survived. Mrs J. J. Hankinson was no longer me. I was Beatrice Hankinson, the milliner who worked as Mrs Faulkner's assistant. This was who I was now, almost twenty-four years old and yet had never had a holiday at the seaside.

But I had more to do before I had a holiday; I had hats to make, and I busied myself once again with the orders I had lined up for the next couple of weeks. Mrs Williams had ordered a hat after coming in last week to buy a new cap for her husband. Then Nora, a very good customer of mine had been in twice to see if her hat was ready; which it wasn't!

"Dear oh dear! Where do I start, Daphne?" I said out loud to the mannequin that stood hatless in the window. I placed my newest plum pink creation at a slight angle on her head. "There, that looks better."

True to his word and against my better judgement, Joe had managed to introduce me to his friend Teddy. He was nice and a lot of fun as Joe had said he was. I tried to not be rude, as I really didn't want the attention, but a small part of me; the young girl, whose first footsteps into love had been overshadowed and destroyed by world affairs, was quite enjoying making new friends. Lizzie had said that I was too young to live a life without love, and a growing part of me couldn't help but agree with that. Perhaps it was time that I make some new friends. There's no harm in that I reasoned. Teddy, Eric and Enoch were quite interesting to talk to, and I did somewhat enjoy listening to their lively conversations. They seemed to have matured from that day when Joe brought them into the shop, and they had acted like children, now we all got on rather well.

Later that evening, I brought the holiday subject up our little gang walked down towards

Moston Brook. A goods train rumbled over the railway bridge as we passed under it, the clattering, as much a part of the familiar noise of life as everything else I knew and loved about this place. The air was warm, and the canal banks were a mass of colour on a carpet of so many shades of green. Yellow dandelions, wood sorrel and cowslips, tiny white daisies, dead nettles, and tall foxgloves adorned the open spaces, but under the trees, masses of tiny blue dayflowers, buttercups and pink spikes of knotweed bloomed. My favourite and sweet little find were the wood violets. John and I used to pick them and taste the sweet perfume of the flowers. I stopped to gather some, smiling to myself at the memory as I nibbled on a petal.

"A holiday? How lovely. I should come with you!" Lizzie said as we stopped our walk on top of Wrigley Head Bridge before the path continued into the thicket on the edge of Moston Brook. I rested myself on the low stone wall and the boys dropped sticks and stones into the canal water. From here I could see the perpetual world of the canal in both directions, with the Oldham to Manchester train track bridge spanning over the canal; trains coming and going, the lifeblood of the wheels of industry pumping through the beating heart of Failsworth. The constant activity that I had always known; shadowy mills and tall chimneys, the heavy-laden barges in continual motion, boatmen shouting to each other, the smell of the horses and the boat wives' washing strung atop the cargo to dry in the warm summer air. The heavy tree branches, stretching out above the water as if trying to reach each other on the opposite side and the dancing lace of light through the leaves, tinkling and shimmering on the path below.

If ever the boats and trains were gone and the canal world be quiet, this place would be a paradise.

Lizzie turned to her friend Jane. "Why don't we all go, we girls, Joe and the boys too? We would have such fun."

Everyone pitched in then with their ideas and we excitedly made plans for a trip to Blackpool when the Wakes week started in August.

"I will have to write to Mrs Fish," I said. "We would need three rooms, we girls in one and two rooms for the boys."

Gusto and eager chatter accompanied the rest of our walk as we discussed the fun, we would all have on our visit to the seaside. Enoch had promised to visit family in the Isle of Man, but Eric had been to Blackpool before and recited to us all that we could expect to see there; the tower, dancing in the ballroom, the winter gardens, the promenade, the sunshine and sea air…

The next few weeks passed swiftly enough that finally, the Sunday morning of our departure arrived and the six of us walked over the old familiar lock bridge, along Old Road and down to the station on Hardman Lane. We could ride this train to Blackpool via Manchester Victoria only three and a half miles away.

As we approached the station, we joined the noisy queue of holidaymakers; a heady mixture of smoke, engine oil and steam assaulted the nostrils, yet only added to our happiness that August morning.

"Which platform?" asked Joe for the tenth time, eagerly looking at his ticket again.

"This way, come on," laughed Teddy, heading off up the stairs above the booking office and on to the Manchester platform. He walked over towards the large green and gold painted beast of an engine sat at the platform gently hissing its steam, like a mythical monster sleeping. There were eight creamy yellow and brown Pullman carriages coupled together behind it, an immense belly, gradually consuming passengers.

I swapped my heavy leather bag over to my other hand again and followed my sister and brother down the platform, where Eric stood holding open the carriage door for us all. I glanced up to see the driver and his young fire man leaning over the edge of the engine footplate, watching the swarming passengers as they buzzed their excited way along the platform as bees into a hive, laden with hatboxes and travelling bags.

They both nodded and smiled at us from high up as we eagerly climbed one by one into the carriage.

"That young fire man has his eye on you Beatrice," teased Lizzie as I lifted my bag up onto the luggage rack above my head before turning to take my intended seat next to Jane.

"He watched you walk all the way down the platform."

I shook my head, wrinkling up my face at her. She looked pale and a little tired as she sat on the opposite seat across from Joe and Teddy. They had brought a pack of playing cards and Teddy was already shuffling the deck as Joe counted out matchsticks to gambol with.

Jane giggled and blushed, as Eric asked if he could sit next to her, stealing into my seat before I had a chance to sit. Lizzie and I exchanged a knowing look with each other as Jane nodded sweetly, flickering her eyes at him in answer.

I finally sat down next to Lizzie and straightened my skirt, admiring the look of my new lace gloves against the fabric of my new dress, a gift from Mrs Faulkener for all my hard work.

The familiar sound of the slamming of carriage doors and the guards' whistle signalled our departure; the strong shunting dragon-like engine pulled away from Failsworth, puffing and chugging. Its mane of silvery steam and black smoke billowing out from the chimney. Slowly thrusting forwards, out into the open-air, gradually picking up speed. The familiar heartbeat of the steam engine, hissing and blowing as it gathered pace, racing towards Manchester and then the countryside, galloping ahead and onwards towards the sea and Blackpool.

It wasn't long before Lizzie laid her head on my shoulder; rocked by the rhythm of the train, I knew she would soon be asleep.

The dark warehouses and dirt of Manchester disappeared in the mist and smoke and the countryside stretched into the far distance as I gazed through the window. Parallel train tracks disappeared off in all different directions; off into the distance to places still unknown to me and as yet unexplored. Hedges and trees flashed by, fields and hills, towns and villages flickered into and out of my view. The beautiful blue of the sky with fluffy white clouds was the backdrop to the drama unfolding before me as we approached the coast.

That first evening, I wrote out at least half a dozen postcards. The first one I wrote was to Ma to tell her we had arrived safely, and then one to Mrs Faulkener. One for Annie at the shop, a couple of my customers, and one for John's sister Elizabeth too. She and I had become excellent friends, and I valued that small piece of him that I could keep. I think we both did.

I chose the cards especially for each person and on our way out the next morning after breakfast, I placed them in the post box at the end of Yorkshire Street.

"We should walk towards the Tower," shouted Joe as he set off briskly with the others and we all obediently followed, Lizzie trailing behind as always. I linked her arm, and we fell into step as we walked down the promenade, admiring all the ladies and their fashionable hats and the shortening dress lengths.

"You won't get me up there," said Jane to the boys as they eagerly joined the queue at the bottom of the tower buildings.

"I'm not sure I want to go up that high either," I agreed. "I would rather sit just here on the front and watch the world go by."

Lizzie laughed, joining the boys in the queue, "watch the hats go by, you mean. Take a day off Beatrice!"

In the end, Lizzie and the boys went into the Tower arcade and Jane and I sat on the front promenade in the sunshine, gazing out over the sands, packed with holidaymakers, and the vast expanse of water before us. Glints of silver sparkled as the ripples caught the sunlight and I lifted my face towards its warmth.

"Oooo, that's lovely," I whispered, more to myself than to Jane. The heat of the sun warmed my face and shoulders and I longed to take my hat off and my gloves and to feel the gentle breeze lift me as it played on my skin. We were quiet for a very long time.

"I wonder what Mrs Fish will make for tea?" murmured Jane finally. I peeked in her direction and realised she had been copying me, closing her eyes and soaking in the sun's warmth.

"Cheese and ham sandwiches, slices of cucumber and cake. Oooo, and a nice cup of fresh tea," I answered slowly with a smile. "How long do you suppose the others will be?"

"I just wondered the same myself. It's half-past two already."

"Goodness, how time does fly. We should walk onto the beach I think."

I stood up and stretched like a cat that had been curled up in the sunniest spot and watched Jane as she did the same. We crossed over to the railings on the front and took the stone steps down onto the sand. Deck chairs with old ladies sat in them dotted around and families with children, playing in the sand, their fathers with their shirt sleeves and trouser legs rolled up as they built sandcastles together, or riding on donkeys, their bells sounding out above the laughter of the children.

We walked towards the edge of the sea, where the water gently lapped the sand, and it was easier to walk. Children stripped to their underclothes splashed happily about. Mothers with babies on their hips, laughing and splashing about too.

Looking around, we could see many grown-ups that had taken off their boots, hats and jackets and were paddling in the water, sheer pleasure on their faces. I looked at Jane and reached up to my head, slowly taking off my hat, I peeled off my hot gloves too and bent to unbutton my boots.

"Beatrice?" Jane said laughing in fake dismay, as I turned to look at her with a mischievous grin on my face. The beach felt soft beneath my feet, a moist sandy and thoroughly lovely feeling between my toes as I wriggled them into the coolness of the sand. Hatless and carefree, I stepped into the water, lifting my skirts to let the coolness lap against my legs. Turning again to Jane, I watched as she did the same, joining me in this childish and wonderfully liberating feeling of newly found nonconformity and forgetting that I had promised Ma that I would behave as a lady.

Karol Darnell

Chapter twenty-two

The green-eyed

monster

"There's a postcard here for you from your friend at work, your other friend Nora and another one from Enoch," Lizzie announced, her voice sharp and brusque, as she walked into the sunny breakfast room. She smiled at Ted and took her seat at the table next to him. He shuffled uncomfortably moving his chair slightly away from her; looking down at his empty teacup; he didn't answer her.

I took the cards from her outstretched hand that she thrust across the table and quickly read what Annie had written, smiling to myself at her words on the back of the jolly card.

> *Dear Beatie,*
> *Sorry not to write before but you will no I am pushed for time. The Mrs is away till Monday. Tommy as got back safe and looks well. I expect you will look like a Turkey Cock. Best love from Annie and Albert.*

"The Mrs!" I laughed. "Mrs Faulkener would be cross if she knew Annie called her the Mrs." I placed the card on the table, happy to hear from Annie that she was busy. The next card was another humorous one with a buxom lady sat on a deckchair.

Full of the happiness of the morning, I flipped it over to read out loud what Enoch had written from Douglas in the Isle of Man.

> *Dear Friend,*
> *How art going on Bety. How is Teddy. Tell him there is rain here.*
> *Enoch*

"There you are Ted, it's raining in the Isle of Man. He should have come with us after all!" I laughed and started to look at the third card smiling at the picture before turning it over.

Don't miss the last train home

Dear loving Beatrice
Just a few lines to say I am glad you are enjoying
yourselves. Wish I were with you darling
Love from all to all duck remember me to all.
From Nora to Beatrice.

"Why did he ask you about Teddy?" interrupted Lizzie crossly.

Ted shuffled about in his chair again and looked very uneasy. I looked at Lizzie and then at Ted.

"Well, I don't know," I admitted, looking at Lizzies scowl. "He didn't ask about anyone else either, did he? That's rather odd."

Ted stood up, almost knocking his chair over in his haste and scurried out of the room, just as Mrs Fish brought in our eggs for breakfast.

"Whoa lad! Where's he off to in such a hurry?" she asked. "He almost knocked the tray out of my hands!"

She set the tray down in front of Lizzie as I sat holding Enoch's and Nora's cards in my hand feeling completely confused. The abruptness of the scene was a complete mystery to me. Lizzie had been acting odd whenever Ted was in the same room, and he was shy and self-conscious with her. Yet he was always nice and kind to everyone else.

Lizzie looked fiercely at me, "why does Enoch think that you and Teddy are courting?" she snapped loudly. Mrs Fish discretely left the room to leave us face to face and the eggs and toast to go cold.

I sat upright and looked back at her with my mouth slightly ajar. "Whatever gives you that impression Liz? I'm not... I'm not courting him!" I stuttered my reply to her angry face as what she said started to make sense to me. "I like Ted, as a friend," I continued. "Does he think there's something more to it?"

"Yes, Beatrice Humphreys - Hankinson. He does!" she spat. "All the boys like you! Everybody likes you! Teddy likes you! Enoch likes you!" She threw four more cards from Enoch at me in her rage.

"Lizzie!" the exclamation left my lips before I could think about it, as she stood up and turned her back on me. I could feel my face and my ears burning in embarrassment. She turned to look out of the window to the street with her arms folded across her chest, her shoulders rigid in anger.

I took a moment to pause before I argued back at her. There was no point in making her temper worse, I had learned that lesson many times before as we were growing up and I had always fallen fowl of her wrath. She was quick-tempered and shouting back would only make it worse.

I waited, grateful of the silence,

"I thought he liked you," I said softly. "He is always awkward in your presence. Can't you see that?"

She didn't answer, she was shaking as she started to sob.

A clattering on the stairs and Joe's playful laughter broke the awkwardness as he burst into the room with Jane and Eric following behind. Lizzie turned back to me, avoiding my questioning gaze, she demurely wiped her eyes to take her seat at the breakfast table again. She refused to look at my face and I guessed that this subject would have to wait until we were alone. I was still embarrassed; I was sure that everyone else in the guest house had heard her shouting at me.

"Pour the tea Beatie,' said Joe as he picked up a piece of toast to butter it. "I'm ravenous!" He hungrily tucked into his breakfast, ignoring in his childlike way, the unease in the room. He looked up at me when he realised that it was quiet, and I hadn't answered.

"What?" He questioned as he stuffed the piece of toast into his mouth, reaching for another with his free hand.

I smiled and shook my head at him, partly to tell him to not ask any more questions and partly to laugh inwardly at the outburst of truthful emotion from my big sister. She had been the most popular of the three of us girls, as we had been

281

growing up. Flirting with all the boys on her way home from school, letting them carry her books, teasing and dallying with any boy that took her fancy. Always the one with lots of friends; constantly the one I turned to in my times of grief, and she seemed more mature than I could ever be. But here she was this morning, acting like a lovesick teenager rather than the twenty-six-year-old woman.

I remembered how she had been with Alex all those years ago and how her jealousy and toying with his love for her, had probably tainted that relationship, slowly frittering away her chance of happiness with him. Now she was envious of me, or rather resentful of what she mistakenly perceived to be the situation. She thought I was interested in the flattery that two young men, friends of Joe's, showed me. I hadn't seen that at all.

I hadn't expected her outburst and decided I would confront Ted later if I could. I needed to know why he was awkward when she was around.

I finally managed to achieve this later in the afternoon. We were walking down the central pier laughing and the boys were fooling around as they always did. The breeze had picked up slightly and everyone was holding onto their hats walking against the onshore gusts. Eric and Jane had sidled off to walk together, hanging back away from the rest of us so that they could be alone together. Joe and Lizzie stopped to look over the railings at the swirling waves beneath us. Ted was walking ahead, and I managed to catch him up.

"Ted, wait for me. What was that about this morning at breakfast?" I asked, deciding to be more direct in my approach. "You seem shy whenever Lizzie is near you. Don't you like her?"

"Uh... oh," was his embarrassed reply. I could tell he didn't want to talk, and he turned away from me. Then he must have thought better of it and stopped walking. Speaking into the wind he said,

"Yes Beatrice. Actually, I do like her... I like her a lot, but I didn't think she would be interested in me because I am only nineteen and she's so much older than me."

"But you talk to me and I'm older too." I reasoned. "Lizzie thinks you're fond of me, but I think she really likes you, Ted. I think she is very upset that you hurry away when she's in the room and don't talk to her the way you talk to me."

"Does she?" he turned to look at me, and a slow smile spread across his face. He looked so relieved, and I wanted to laugh. I bit my lip and looked up at his youthful expression.

I knew that face, the face of hope and expectation. I had worn that face too before I was broken. When I had lifted my heart from my chest and happily given it to a man who had taken it to war with him. It lay in the cold soil far away now with him and I had slowly learned to live without it.

I could see hope in Ted's eyes, and I had seen that in my sisters' eyes earlier too, back in our room after breakfast, when I had managed to calm her, and she had told me about her true feelings for Ted.

"Why don't you talk to her Ted? You would make her very happy."

I watched him walk away, further down the pier and away from me at first. He stopped to light a cigarette bending his head and shielding the match flame against the wind, he then looked over to where Lizzie and Joe were standing. He slowly approached the pair and Joe looked over to me. I beckoned him over to me, leaving Lizzie and Ted together at last.

Joe and I walked back down the pier towards the Pavilion theatre, losing sight of the others as we pushed ourselves through the throngs of people.

"Come on Joe, let's go and find a cup of tea." I said as I linked my brother's arm and marched him along the pier.

All holidays must end, and I packed the postcards into my bag along with several sticks of Blackpool rock and placed my hat firmly on my head. I looked at myself in the round mirror that stood atop the small dresser in our room. I looked rested and my face had colour from the sea breeze, sunshine and rest. I looked around the little room once more and followed Lizzie and Jane down the stairs.

"Remember me to Mrs Ward and to Mrs Ashton," shouted Mrs Fish as she waved us off. We all shouted our thanks for such lovely hospitality and fell into step with each other as we walked towards the station.

Once again, the train stood at the platform, hissing patiently; waiting for us all to clamber on board and I looked up at the great shiny beast with huge wheels, coupling rods and pistons: a masterpiece of engineering driven by the basic elements of fire and water.

The same lad, the fireman that had brought us here was leaning out of the engine cab window watching the crowds as they once again loaded into the carriages.

I caught his gaze as he smiled at me and this time, relaxed and happier for my holiday, I smiled back. He had a lovely smile and in that moment there was calm. I thought about his smile all the way home. His face was grubby with soot from the fire and there were white lines around his eyes where he must have wrinkled his face against the heat as he stoked the huge fire with great shovelfuls of coal. He wore a dirty off-white fireman's flat cap and a blue boiler suit that was as grimy as his face with coal dust.

"What are you smiling about?" questioned Joe. "We're going home, back to work and that's now't to smile about."

Distracted, I gazed out of the window to watch the sea disappear out of view; secretly knowing I would come this way again.

It was nice to see other people falling in love and making plans for the future, as I had once done. Although my memories were tinged with longing and sadness, it was nice to see Lizzie and Ted getting to know each other. They were sometimes still a little awkward with each other, but I thought Lizzie was trying her best not to make a mess of it this time. Ted was cautious with her, young and inexperienced in how to treat a lass; but somehow, they were managing to make it work and Lizzie was a happier girl for it.

Time passed; work and life carried on as it always did in Failsworth. Winter came and went, then spring gave way to summer. Joe and the boys decided that they should go on holiday together this year and almost as soon as they had gone, a postcard arrived from him. Ma took one look at it and handed it to Lizzie with a despairing yet humorous look on her face.

"I rather wish you had gone with them Beatrice. I do worry what trouble the boys could get up to when left alone."

"He's a big boy now Ma, and besides, Teddy will keep him in check. I've given strict instructions." said Lizzie as she read the card. Her face was pale and there were dark rings under her eyes. She was sick again and wasn't working at the moment but the foreman of Lees Brothers at the Albert Mill, Hollinwood said he would take her back when she felt well enough again. She rocked slowly on the rocking chair in front of the fire. It was much too warm for a fire, but it had to stay lit for cooking and Lizzie said she would doze off for hours at a time. She said she didn't miss being a creeler at all.

"If I never see another spindle and shuttle, it will be a day too soon," she said, yawning as I took the card from her to read it myself.

I snickered at the picture on the card and flipped it over to read what he had written in his usually messy scrawling handwriting.

Cooke Street lads are here
Teddy on front enjoying himself
Dear Sisters,

I write these few lines to let you know we have got the trolly and we are enjoying ourselves at the places so that is all at present xxxx Goodbye Joe.

I placed the card on the mantelpiece above the fire, knowing full well it would be in my box before the week was out. And sat down at the table, pouring myself more tea.

Ma placed two pieces of bread on the table in front of me that she had toasted on the fire, I spread a thin layer of her home-made blackberry jam on them both and handed Lizzie a piece. The bittersweet taste filled my mouth and the crispness of the toast felt so very good on my tongue. I savoured the tang, washing it down with my last mouthful of tea before rising from the table.

"Well, I'm off to the shop," I said, kissing Ma on her cheek, "What are you going to be doing today Ma?"

"It's Wednesday and the lady's afternoon at the New Jerusalem Church. I thought I would take one of Joe's poems with me to recite."

"Which one, he's written so many?"

The canal in snow one. It's simply lovely."

She cleared her throat and started to recite Joe's poem:

"Mallard green and earth brown mud,
Melting puddles where once I stood
On swan white snow, underfoot crisp,
Nose drips; breath, a steamy wisp.

Silver moon in clear black sky,
Cold dark echo as barn owls cry,
Barges glow, warm lanterns hung,
Travellers' music softly sung.

Fingerless gloves on work-tired hands
That move the snow as it quietly lands,
Crank the lock gates to open the flow,
No rest for the boatmen with far to go."

Lizzie and I both clapped our hands at her performance.

"Beautiful," I said as I walked out of the door. "The ladies will love it."

His poem rang through my head as I walked to work. That particular one made me think of the canal life I knew so well, and how bitter the winters seem, when it was so sultry and clammy this August day. He had caught exactly the canal in winter and the never-ending motion of the barges, the families that lived on them and travelled perpetually up and down with their goods from the hills to the docks and back again.

I smiled at so many memories of my life here in Failsworth that I arrived at the shop before I knew it.

"Mornin' Beatie," sang Annie as she handed yet another postcard to me. This one was from Eric on holiday on the Wirral.

> *17 Alderley Road, Hoylake 25/8/21*
> *Dear Beatrice*
> *I hope you are quite well and enjoying yourself in*
> *dirty old Failsworth. The weather is mixed.*
> *With love from me (Eric) to you in Failsworth*

Poor Eric: his relationship with Jane hadn't gone anywhere, ending up as a holiday infatuation for them both, but he had kept in touch with me which was nice, and Lizzie found that acceptable. I placed the card on the shelf behind me with all the others I had received from friends and customers and drew a deep breath as I looked around the shop. The whole place looked a jumble and I needed to dust the window display. There were boxes on the floor and a delivery of fabrics expected this morning.

Where to start? I thought. Where to start indeed.

Chapter twenty-three

Emma and

Thomas

Days gallop by and weeks become months. My work at the shop was all-consuming, and I enjoyed every minute. Lizzie had returned to work, as did Joe, and Christmas that year came and went in a flicker of time that passed with little comment yet again. We are a more subdued family these days and Christmases pass only to invoke memories of all those we have loved and lost along the way. It is sometimes hard to feel cheer; Eunice, Pa, Granny and Grandpa Ward and Granny Humphreys, all long gone; as was my dearest husband John, my love, my JJ.

Wounds run deep and I know I will never love again, although Lizzie tells me I will. She and Ted have been courting for almost a year now and often go out to The Grand picture house on Oldham Road whenever she was well.

"What did you go to see this time?" I asked, barely interested as I was reading my latest book, 'La Gitanilla'.

"The Bohemian Girl," answered Lizzie, yawning. "It's about a girl called Arline, played by Gladys Cooper, who was a princess but becomes a gipsy and she falls in love with Ivor Novello, another gipsy... Thaddeus - oh it's too complicated, you need to go to see it yourself."

"That's the same plot as my book!" I replied. "The gipsy queen loves Thaddeus too and plots to destroy Arline."

"Yes, that's it. They arrest Arline for telling fortunes...and there's a stolen medallion...or something, and she finds her long-lost father, the Count Arnheim... or someone."

"Well, I simply must see that film. I love Gladys Cooper. Do you remember, Lizzie, she was Eunice's favourite too?"

"I'll come with you," chirped Ma. "We could go tomorrow evening if you like. Are you coming too, Joe?"

He groaned to have to come with us to see a romance, but the following evening the three of us walked over to the picture house and joined the queue to buy our tickets. We each gave our pennies to Joe, who presented them to a pretty girl with dark curly hair who was sitting in the office box selling the tickets.

Out of the corner of my eye, I watched him. He lingered to talk to her; she smiled at him as they chatted and as she handed the three tickets to Joe; she nodded her head and blushed slightly.

"I know that girl," he said as he turned back to us, and we followed Ma through the doors into the darkened cinema where the film was to be shown. "She's called Emma. Her sister Clara Butt was in my class at school. I thought I recognised her. Isn't she pretty Ma?"

That was all I needed to tell me that my soppy little brother was love-struck. The thought warmed me throughout the film, the flickering pictures and dialogue cards jumbling in my head as I watched Joe's dreamy face rather than the characters telling the story of the gipsy girl, Arline on the silver screen. I knew he wasn't watching the film either and I could see that look on his face, his flat cap pulled over his eyes as he dragged on his cigarette, blowing the smoke out through lips puckered into a kiss.

I knew he was thinking of Emma.

Within three weeks, he had found her again; she lived at 20 Norman Street, and she worked at Ferranti Electrical as a machine hand. Her father, Thomas William, was a mechanical engineer at Ferranti too. The fifth of seven children, Emma, also worked at the cinema for extra pocket money whenever she could.

She was indeed a sweet and pretty girl and she and I got on rather well. I could tell she liked Joe, but something was troubling her. She seemed tense and edgy sometimes when Joe asked to see her again. I couldn't understand the deep and uneasy feeling I had, and it disturbed me. Joe seemed oblivious to this little inkling that I had, and he continued to see her, taking her out whenever he could and it looked, on the surface at least, that the promising buds of love were blossoming indeed.

These romances being nurtured at South View both entertained and troubled me in equal measure. There were constant comings and goings, lively and happy debate, and great friendships being developed between us all; but Lizzie's health was a significant concern to me and one evening as I sat brushing my hair, I looked over to her and noticed that her long locks were looking lank and greying at the roots as she plaited her hair ready for bed. She looked around at me watching her and I saw the fatigue on her face.

"Can you hear a ringing noise, Beatie?" she asked, dropping her long thin plait from her shaky fingers.

"No, I heard an owl earlier, though." I climbed into bed and beckoned her to me. I patted the bed next to me. "Sleep here tonight, Lizzie, you don't look well."

"I'm cold," she looked confused as I blew out the candle whilst she climbed into bed.

"I'll keep you warm," I promised. I wrapped my arms around her thin shoulders and placed a kiss on her forehead. She yawned and was asleep within minutes; her feet snug in a little pair of knitted socks that Joe had made for her, and a shawl wrapped around her. I smiled at the memories I had of when we were younger. Eunice, Lizzie and me, all sat cross-legged on the floor, teaching Joe how to knit in the flickering firelight of a winter's evening, while Ma rocked in the rocking chair helping us when we each dropped a stitch or needed help to cast on or off. Fancy stitches were tried, and we had little competitions with each other to see who could knit the fastest. Lizzie always won, of course, but Joe frequently came a very close second; while Eunice and I dropped more stitches, trying far too hard to keep up. These particular socks were a joint effort between Joe and Lizzie; she knitted one and he the other until they ran out of blue wool and Joe's sock had to be finished in a garish green wool that didn't match very well at all.

"They are snug, and I love them," Lizzie had stated, wriggling her toes in them.

The full moon was bright tonight, daggers of silver light piercing through the gaps in the curtains and into the darkness of the tiny room. The China doll that Eunice had loved so much sat on the chest of drawers in a shaft of moonlight; her ragged dress, illuminated and still.

Up in his attic room, I could hear Joe's bothersome yet familiar snoring. I heard his bed's well-known creak as he turned in his sleep, and all was quiet.

I must have drifted off to sleep, as I know I dreamed of John again. He gently covered my face with his, his lips on mine, soft yet demanding. I stirred to feel his hardness enter me, and my body warmed at his touch; I moved again to push against him and felt the emptiness that was real. I searched in my dreams for him, but he was nowhere.

The next morning, I could not shake that empty feeling that I woke up with. The day at the shop was long and filled with a certain tedium that I could not explain. Not that I would have wanted to describe how I felt to anyone, as I barely understood it myself. Suffice it to say I was unsettled and whereas, for a very long time, I had felt that my life was getting better, with new friends and happiness for Lizzie with Teddy and Joe with his young love Emma; I was hollow.

I scurried home as soon as the shop clock showed six, hardly saying a word of goodbye to Mrs Faulkener; nor my usual cheery "hello" to Ma as I took off my hat and heaved myself into the rocking chair.

My all-knowing, kind, understanding, and unflappable Ma passed me a freshly brewed cup of tea and said nothing until at least fifteen minutes had elapsed. Finally, she spoke.

"I've seen that boy come down the alley and pass the house again, Beatrice. That's three times this week."

"Which boy?" I asked, with little interest at all.

"I don't know who he is, but he has a cheek, loitering as if he's looking for someone."

"Who Ma?" I asked again rather crossly.

"There's a young man in dirty blue overalls and a mucky cap, who walks down the alley from Ellesmere Street and then lingers outside the house before disappearing up Wrigley Head," she repeated. "Every night this week, three nights on the trot."

"Maybe he's looking for Joe." I dismissed the thoughts that ran through my head. "I've never seen him." I rested my head against the chair back, closed my eyes and rocked.

Ma shrugged and stirred the stew pot that was bubbling away for tea before walking outside to bring in the washing that had been on the line all day, drying in the breeze.

"He's there again Beatrice," she said, over the bundle of dry clothes in her arms as she came back inside. "Go out and see what he wants. Will you please, love?"

I sighed and tutted under my breath. Not wanting to go outside, rather wanting to dwell on my thoughts and rest my weary feet, but I thought better of defying an order from Ma. This boy hanging about was obviously troubling her and so I reluctantly removed Tinker from my lap and got up from the rocking chair. I blinked as I went out through the front door into the late summer sunshine.

I knew him instantly. He was leaning on the side wall of the house opposite, with one leg bent so that his foot rested on the wall under his buttocks. He grabbed his dirty cap from his head and jumped up to stand straight as I approached him.

"There you are," he said. "I've been looking for you ever since I saw you at the station last year, only I didn't know your name. I thought I saw you last week on my way home from work."

"Have you been following me?" I asked. My irritation of the day wouldn't leave me.

"Yes," he sounded excited. "I'm glad I found you."

"Well, now you have!" I thought about turning around and going back inside, but his smile stopped me, and I waited.

"I'm Thomas," he announced. "Thomas Rowland."

I reached out politely to shake his outstretched hand.

"I'm... Beatrice Hankinson... well, I was Humphreys before I was married... but he died in the war." That sounded so matter of fact, so awkward and distant, I wanted to change the subject quickly. "Where do you live?"

Looking at his blue eyes unnerved me, and I didn't want to get emotional. That was what was wrong with me. I was feeling emotional today, and I needed to shake off that feeling.

"Robert Street, Newton Heath, but I drive my train through Failsworth every day, unless I am put on the seaside shifts at Wakes week. I will pull the whistle for you tomorrow, so you know it's me when I go over Wrigley Head Bridge," he laughed.

I matched his grin and felt the tension of the day start to lift. The sun had moved over now. It was chilly in the alleyway, and I didn't have my shawl.

"I'm sorry, are you cold?" he asked. "We could walk if you like."

I hesitated for a moment, "I would have to get my shawl," I replied as I turned away to go inside. Ma was busying herself in the kitchen.

"I'm going for a walk, Ma," I shouted. "I won't be long."

By the time I got back, it was almost dark, and I was rather happy to have made a new friend but although my mood of the day had lifted, I felt a pang of guilt that I had never experienced before. A sense of grief and loss that I ought not to be so happy; and that surprised me.

We had walked up Wrigley Head, and I had shown Thomas the cottage where my Grandpa Ward used to live; I told him tales of our childhood and of Eunice and John. He listened to my ramblings, and I found that both comforting and therapeutic. He told me about his job as a steam train driver and how his father was a railway waggon inspector. He had three brothers and three sisters, and we chattered away as if we were old-time friends. He told me that he had dozens of twenty-first birthday cards in a box under his bed and I laughed and told him about my now very tatty box holding all my precious postcards and birthday cards, and how it was now overflowing.

We walked on, not down the canal this time, but turning right at the top of Wickentree Lane. Crossing over Oldham Road, we wandered along Norman Street. I almost didn't see Emma until the last minute. I was so engaged in conversation with Thomas and thinking about it now; I realise she was trying to avoid being seen by me.

She stepped back behind a tree and then I saw a dark-haired boy that she had been rather too close to, step away too. He looked around at us as we strolled past.

"Hello, Emma,"

"Er... hello Beatie," she replied, looking shocked to have been seen and so I carried on walking past rather than stopping to talk to her, as I might have done in a less awkward moment.

Thinking no more about it, Thomas and I carried on walking, turning right into Minor Street and then back towards Oldham Road via Shepley Street to saunter home, chattering as if we had known each other for years.

He dipped his head towards me in a simple polite gesture as he left me by the door and asked if I might be interested in walking out again sometime.

Perhaps my instant and happy, "yes please," egged him on but I realised that I wanted to see him again and, despite the guilty niggle, I was pleased indeed as I went back inside for my tea.

I mentioned to Joe that I had seen Emma with another boy, then instantly realised I had said too much.

"She told me she was working," he scowled. "That's why she couldn't see me tonight."

"Before you go accusing her of anything, I think you should tread carefully," interjected Ma from the kitchen sink. "It could be perfectly innocent."

"Perhaps Ma's right Joe," I said. "Be careful to not upset her."

But the next evening, as I came home from work, Emma was already at our house and was waiting for me rather than Joe.

"Oh Beatie, I'm in an awful mess. I really like your Joe," she had started to cry and between sobs, Ma and I managed to get the story out of her that there was a lad at Ferranti who was very keen on her and he followed her home and pestered her to go out with him. So, despite her seeing our Joe, she had not been strong enough to refuse him. Last evening when I had walked past her, she had been trying to tell him she didn't want to see him anymore and that she wanted to see Joe, but he was being rather persuasive.

"Oh Beatie!" she cried. "Mrs Ward… he gave me this and wouldn't take it back." She was sobbing into her handkerchief now, her face red and as she unfurled her fingers, she showed us a little engagement ring in her palm.

"He wouldn't listen." She wailed. "And now Joe is mad at me too. What should I do?"

I placed my arm around Emma's shoulders and looked at Ma's amused expression.

"Well, if he won't take it back, you will have to keep it," stated Ma, her female astuteness at the fore. "But you do get to choose which lad you give your heart to, love."

Emma stopped snivelling and looked up at me. "I never thought of it like that," she sniffed. "I didn't know what to do, I thought I had to marry him when he gave me the ring. Of course, I have a choice, I can. see that now; you have a lovely family, Mrs Ward and Joe makes me feel so special."

Karol Darnell

Chapter twenty-four

Comings and goings

Christmas was a lot more fun with a houseful of people. Thomas, Emma and Ted were all frequent visitors and seeing Ma laughing and talking to our new friends was pleasantly amusing. Everybody was happy, and that was refreshing and fun. Joe and Emma had worked out their differences, Joe being so very forgiving of Emma's naivety that she grew in confidence in the few short months that they had been seeing each other.

Thomas took me to his home too and introduced me to his father, Joseph and stepmother Emma, and it was only then that he told me that his own mother, Mary Ann had died when he was fourteen and that his father had remarried. It also explained the two youngest children running around our feet giggling happily. Thomas picked up the youngest; a three-year-old also called Emma and swung her over his shoulder. She giggled in that secure and trusting way that young children have.

"There are too many Emma's here!" he said, laughing. "I might throw this one into the dustbin."

The child squealed and wriggled out of his arms; running off to hide behind her other brothers Cyril and Joseph who were playing with a toy train set on the floor of the kitchen. She peeped up at me, a newcomer into their home, with the inquisitiveness of a nervous kitten wanting to take the morsel of food from an outstretched hand.

His sisters, Annie & Edith were sitting at the kitchen table peeling potatoes for our meal.

"Train mad the lot of them," Annie said as she briefly looked up to say hello to me. "Norman will be back from work soon and then we can eat." Norman also worked at the railway yard on Dean Lane with Thomas and their father.

The meal was delicious, and I heard all about driving trains and the goods yard and how a steam engine worked from Thomas' eager brothers and sisters and by the time I had helped with the washing up, I knew more about trains and steam engines than I ever thought possible. The nervous kitten, Emma, finally at ease enough to sit on my knee with her picture book whilst we all chattered away.

Thomas walked me home later that evening. We walked slowly and I could tell he wanted to hold my hand as his arm brushed mine several times, but I stuffed my gloved hands inside my pockets and tried to hurry the pace. It was cold and there was a bitter wind, and a brisk walk would have been the warmer option, but Thomas slowed us down at each street corner. I scurried on. He lingered longer than he ought to outside our front door, waiting for what I knew was his expectation of perhaps a kiss. I turned away after thanking him for a lovely time with his family. I couldn't get close. I simply couldn't. I enjoyed his company, and he made my heart feel a little lighter, but I still couldn't bring myself to stand too near him, nor look up into his gentle eyes. I couldn't stand close to him long enough quite - so that he might lean down and peck me on the cheek; or closer still - goodness me no! I couldn't!

I turned to walk away, and I felt his eyes watch me as I closed the front door behind me. Tears prickled behind my eyelids and my heart hurt, for loss and happiness in conflict with each other. I breathed a deep sigh and stiffened myself against my thoughts as I entered the kitchen where Ma sat on the rocking chair. Joe and Emma on the floor at her feet.

"Have you had a nice time?" asked Ma. "Lizzie has gone up to bed already."

Joe and Emma didn't even look up; Emma chattering away as always and Joe listening with a sentimental look on his face, watching her with his puppy dog eyes completely entranced and yet, I knew, not really listening to her.

"My dad was in Barrow-in-Furness in the war, working on the submarines. When he came back Mr Ferranti said he could be a cleaner in the factory, but my dad said he was too good for that, he's an engineer you know. Joe, are you listening?"

"Mmmm," he murmured in reply.

He held the long handled toasting fork above the flames, toasting a piece of bacon for his supper. The grease crackled and sizzled and dripped down the front of the grate. Laddie lay with his head on Emma's lap, watching with intent, the piece of bacon, in case it fell from the fork.

I smiled at Ma, she was trying hard not to laugh at Joe, and I had to look away too for chance we gave the game away.

"Yes, it was very pleasant," I replied, biting my lip. I took off my hat and gloves and unbuttoned my coat turning to hang it as always on the wooden peg behind the door. I picked up Joe's coat from where it had landed, as always on the floor.

"Well, as I was saying Joe, our Clara wanted to go dancing and my dad wouldn't let her. Well, she kicked up a fuss she did, she stormed out of the house and walked down the street with our dad shouting at her to get back home, little madam! Well, our Ernest and our Frank were egging her on and our Ada was crying!"

She continued, hardly stopping to draw breath. "Well, the next night, guess what? She gave me a penny so that I would drop her dancing shoes out of the bedroom window to her. She crept out of the house and Dad never knew that's where she was going! Isn't she a minx Joe?"

"Yes," he murmured in a dreamy reply. "You don't half confuse me with your tales Emma. I can't keep track of all these brothers and sisters you have!"

She thumped him on the arm with her fist in playful jest. "Oh Joe! You just don't listen!"

The eldest is our Lewis, he got shrapnel in his shoulder at Passchendaele, then our Lillian who's married and expecting her first, and then our Ernest, he's also married, our Clara who loves dancing. Then me," she stopped to finally draw breath but quickly continued. "Then our Frank, there was Margaret the baby... but she died and then our Ada, she's only 11 and still at school."

"Perhaps I should write a poem with all their names in, so I won't forget them," he laughed.

"I'm off up to bed," said Ma, suppressing yet another giggle. The rocking chair creaked as she stood up and I followed her upstairs, leaving the chattering lovebirds alone with their bacon supper.

Day by day the winter passed. There were weeks of rain with dark cloudy skies and strong winds where the roof tiles chattered like an old mans' teeth. The bitter northern wind would penetrate my clothes and strike right through to the bone, so much so that it was hard to keep warm and difficult to stitch or fashion the many hats I had to make.

Yet, as always there was the pledge of spring ahead, and eventually the days lengthened. Many were sunny days that started fresh with an unfulfilled promise of warmth later; and many frosty mornings that turned out to be warm and sweet days. Bright daffodils gave way to swathes of bluebells and the perky white stars of wood anemone down by the canal. Moston brook was filled with the heady scent of early summer. Lesser celandine yellow, dandelions and bright white daisies sprinkled like spilled buttons on the carpet of the riverbank. Tall spires of purple honesty, my favourite flower that held so many memories, and hawthorn blossom, creamy white tentative brush strokes on the hedgerows, newly splashed with dots of green. Fresh lime, jade and emerald leaf buds uncurling, springing from unidentified twigs and branches, in an age-old sequence that filled the thickets with colour; each tree now regaining their own identity and purpose. Diligent bees and hover flies, tiny beetles busying themselves in a fury and commitment known only to them. Peckish birds picking up twigs and leaf litter, moss and cotton fluff that had flown from the mills to prepare nests for their future egg laying and later hatchlings. Each tiny creature, meticulously following their own life plan without thinking, and without question or care. Ordained through creation to their course and obligation to life, as we are also driven.

Ma spent many hours down at the allotment; digging and sowing her carefully gathered seed, planting her prizewinning potatoes, gathering spring greens and reddening stalks of forced rhubarb for the table. In our youth we would help her much more, but now Joe and I were busy working and Lizzie, well, Lizzie was always too tired. Her face so pale and wan some days.

"I might visit Aunt Emily again this summer," Lizzie mused one evening in early June. "I think the fresher air may make me feel better."

"That reminds me girls, a postcard came from Aunt Mary earlier," Shouted Ma from the kitchen sink where she was washing greenfly from an early lettuce and a handful of spring onions.

"Yes, I saw it, Ma," Lizzie answered. "Teddy is coming back later to collect me, and we will go to meet her at the station."

I picked up the card. The Welsh lady's hat opened out and inside was a concertina of pictures of the area around Llangollen.

"That's a nice card," I said, carefully folding the tiny pictures back into the hat. "I should like to go further over into Wales this year. Thomas wants to take me to Rhyl on the North Wales coast." I kneeled on the pegged hearth rug and pushed Laddie out of the way so that I could sit on the footstool to unbutton my boots.

"I don't have the money for a holiday," Joe said as he grabbed up his jacket from the floor. He flashed a smile at Ma and me and hurried out to meet Emma.

"I'll leave your tea on a plate, shall I?" Ma shouted after him, laughing to herself, that in his haste, Joe had forgotten to eat.

"I'm not sure I want to go with him," I continued, more to myself than to Lizzie and Ma. "He's trying to court me, and I'm not sure I can be more than a friend."

My comments went unanswered in the chaos of a Saturday night's teatime, but later that evening when Lizzie and I were getting ready for bed, she picked up on what I had been saying earlier.

"Why can't you be more than a friend to Thomas, Bea?" she asked. "He's very fond of you and I thought you liked him too."

I looked over to her and sighed.

I could bear my soul to Lizzie; she always knew what was in my heart.

"I can't, I... I feel as if I am being unfaithful to JJ," there! I had said it. I had finally worked out what it was that had been making me so unsure about my feelings for Thomas. There had been no funeral for John, no ending, and no final goodbye. I was a widow, but I still longed for him to come home.

"I'm not sure," I repeated. "How can I love him and forget John? How can I love anyone else? Everyone I ever loved was taken away from me. I don't know if I can... it hurts too much."

"Let it happen Bea," she said. "Let love happen." It was a simple statement and the logic to it was very clear but that didn't stop me feeling what I did, and I told her so.

"Beatrice, Beatrice, my darling little sister. Life is so short for so many of us, and love is so hard to find and to keep hold of. You should know that much at least."

I agreed by nodding my head and taking the hands that she reached out to me. Her fingers were thin and her touch quite light and weak. She pulled me to sit beside her on the bed.

"Live for me Beatrice, love for the both of us."

"Whatever do you mean Lizzie?" I asked, a sob caught in my throat as her words impacted on me.

"I feel weak… I feel tired… I am ill, Bea, … I want to live and yet I don't think I can for much longer. Pernicious Anaemia is not something anyone can recover from, you know. Please don't be upset because I shall marry Teddy and I will try to stay alive. I just don't want to think that you will be alone when I'm gone. You are young; you are fit and well, and you have another chance to be happy. Don't miss that chance."

Her frail body was shaking as we sat side by side with our arms wrapped around each other, sobbing and rocking until the candle, snuffed out by a draft from the open window, spluttered out and it was quite dark.

The clock downstairs ticked slowly, holding back the time; counting the seconds as slowly as it was able. I shivered and stood to help Lizzie into bed.

"The unveiling of the cenotaph is tomorrow afternoon," she yawned. "We are still going, aren't we?"

"Yes, we are. I must be at the Popular Picture Palace at two o'clock with the other widows ready for the procession. It's the only thing I can do for John now; I just hope it helps me and I don't get too upset. Elizabeth Chappell has been invited to do the unveiling. Poor woman, she lost four of her sons including Ernest, Leah's husband."

"Oh, of course, I forgot, Janie Melling's sister Leah. We should be glad Joe was too young to go and fight. I can't bear to think..."

"Hush Lizzie, don't cry," I begged as I watched a large tear slide from her eye in the darkness, the feint light from the window, picking it out as it glistened and trickled down the side of her face to disappear into her hair. "I will let Thomas take me to Rhyl, Lizzie," I whispered as I covered us both up, tucking the covers around her thin shoulders. "I will try to let myself love him. Sleep now, we have tomorrow to get through first. We will make our holiday plans as soon as we are able."

She smiled at me in the semi- darkness, a most lovely, sweet and strong smile. A smile that was just for me, and we slept like babies, wrapped in each other's arms until morning.

Karol Darnell

Chapter twenty-five

Another train

journey

Rhyl was everything Thomas told me it would be and more besides. The air was fresh, and I could smell the sea from my small room at The Leinster guesthouse on the High Street. The bed was the most comfortable I have ever slept in, soft and cosy with four large feather pillows all to myself. There was a small sofa covered in the prettiest chintz fabric and curtains to match, whilst the eiderdown and coverlet on the bed was a soft pink. The chest of drawers and nightstand matched the wardrobe and were a light oak colour; and there was a little cast iron, blacked and polished fireplace with a basket of dried flowers arranged in the grate. The morning after we arrived, I stood looking out of the open window in my pretty bedroom, my hands on the sill. If I leaned out, I could see the sea and the warm sunshine made me feel very eager indeed to start the day. I closed the sash again and hurried downstairs, the familiar and appealing smell of bacon wafted up to greet me.

Thomas's room overlooked the back of the property, and he couldn't see the sea at all; although he said he had a great view of Mrs Lunn's vegetable garden.

"I knew you would prefer that room, it's bright and sunny," he said as he passed the strawberry jam to me at breakfast.

"I hope you have left me some jam!" I laughed, pointing to the copious amount he had lavished on his toast. "I do, thank you. I think it's a simply charming bedroom."

"As lovely as strawberry jam on toast?"

"Twice as sweet," I agreed with a flash of a smile.

"We should buy some postcards this morning to let everyone know we have arrived," he suggested. "The post office is only just across the road, and we can have a walk to the sea front if you like."

"That would be lovely," I nodded in agreement, I longed to see the sea again; I hadn't seen it since my holiday in Blackpool, two summers ago.

"There's something about the sea that makes me feel so small," I mused out loud. "It's so vast. I should like to sail away on a large ocean liner and visit faraway lands."

Thomas raised his eyebrows in mock surprise at my statement. "Leave Failsworth?"

"Well, no, I couldn't leave Failsworth, but it might be nice to go to new places and send postcards home."

"It's all about postcards to you, isn't it?" he laughed. "Postcards to keep in your box. Your Ma told me that if a card comes to your house, within three days it has disappeared upstairs to the box under your bed."

"Guilty as charged, your honour," I giggled with pretend guilt and held up my hands. "Although my box is rather full and tatty now. I was eying up a discarded hat box in the shop last week, but Mrs Faulkener used it before I could ask her if I could have it."

"That's too bad," he tutted and reached for the teapot to pour some more tea. He quickly drained his cup and wiped his mouth on his napkin. "Are we ready then?"

I stood up and folded my napkin, placing it on the table and we walked out into the August sunshine, heading towards the post office where I chose a card to send to Ma.

"I wager, you'll put that in your box when you get home too," Thomas teased.

"I probably will," I agreed with a chuckle, and said I would help him to choose one to send to his family too. We began to search through the racks of postcards, standing side by side.

"Here's one," he said, holding out a card, it was the same one that I had just picked up. We smiled at each other as we looked at the same jolly card with a cartoon of people rushing to climb into a train carriage. The slogan across the top said,

'Don't miss the last train home'.

"Perfect," we agreed in unison.

We wandered along to the busy sea front, walking until we found an empty bench where we could write out our cards, looking out over the water.

"I wonder what's out there?" I questioned out loud. "The sea is so beautiful. There must be some lovely places to visit."

"There are Beatrice," he said, looking earnestly at me. "I see some wonderful sights when I'm up in the cab of the engine. Hills and lakes, great mountains and forests."

"Do you?" I asked surprised, sitting up to look at him. "I didn't know you went that far. I thought you were based at Dean Lane and mostly saw the goods yards and engine sheds of Newton Heath and Manchester. All engine oil, waggons full of coal and lumber and steam!"

"I do mostly," he agreed seriously, a slow dreamy smile twitched at the edge of his lips. "But in my dreams, I see many places I might like to visit. I imagine I am travelling far away, to the places I see and read about in books."

I laughed at him then. He reminded me of Joe, pensive and artistic; a little of John too, imaginative, and playful; bursting with aspirations and daydreams of the places he would like to travel to. Above all I recognised myself in him, and that made me feel secure.

"What are you going to write on your card?" I asked.

"To all, Having a nice time. Thomas and Beatrice. I'm keeping it brief." He answered with a twinkle in his eye, and we laughed together like children.

I showed him my card of a lady sat on a rock on the beach. Printed on the front were the words,

I'm having a really nice time But I haven't forgotten you for all that

On the back I wrote.

> *Dear Ma*
> *We have arrived quite safe & are enjoying*
> *ourselves fine. Mr & Mrs Lunn are quite well.*
> *Best wishes to all*
> *Beaty & Thomas*

We sat for a while in the sunshine until Thomas took out his pocket watch, that hung from a fob chain on his waistcoat.

"Come on, I have a surprise for you," he stood up and started to walk away.

"We need to post these cards," I said as we were walking back towards High Street, but he carried on past the end of that street and turned left into Queen Street heading towards the train station rather than the post office.

"Where are you going?" I said, having to trot a little to catch up with him.

"I told you I have a surprise."

We boarded the train and took our places but still he wouldn't tell me where we were going, even when the train puffed its way out of the station and headed west.

"I want to show you the coastline, and a magical castle," he explained once the train had gathered speed. Great cliffs and crags rose on our left and the sea, stretched away to the right of us. We galloped past little farms and a castle hidden in the trees.

"That's Gwydr castle," he said as we sped along. "There's a better one further on."

I gasped. Steep embankments that were very close to us at times; it seemed as if we were travelling over the water as we headed towards Colwyn Bay, a great sweep of a beach. The train paused to take on more passengers at Colwyn station before heading away from the coast a little, so it seemed we were heading inland. Then almost instantly the sea appeared before us again.

That's when I saw it! Immediately before us rose a magnificent castle and the train charged towards it as if it were a flying black horse.

"It's from a romantic novel," I inhaled in childlike awe, surveying the turrets as they loomed closer and closer before us, my nose pressed against the glass so that I could see better. The monstrous train panted as it slowed to carry us under a tunnel; the whistle blew, and the roar of the engine exploded in my ears as we disappeared into what appeared to be the castle itself and then out at the other side; the thick walls and castellations towering high above us as we steamed on our way, as close on our right as it could ever be possible to be. Thomas watched my excited face with amusement.

"Wasn't that wonderful?" he enthused, as eager as I was. I could only nod with the thrill of it all.

To the left was a small inlet of water with tiny fishing boats moored on their sides on the sand, waiting for the tide to come in and fill the inlet with water so that the little boats could bob once more. Under and over stone bridges we glided in our giant chariot. To the left, the castle walls continued around the little town of Conwy, guarding the sleepy place from some great enemy, and lost in the mystery of time. Onwards and away past great hillsides and crags once more.

"On the other side of this great hill is the Scynant pass," said Thomas. "I should like to explore there one day."

"I have a postcard from there," I told him. "Some friends sent Ma a card some years ago. Yes, I remember now. They were staying in Llandudno, and they walked to Scynant Pass. I always wondered where it was," I beamed at him, and we both said, almost in harmony, "It's in my box!"

The sea came into view again and across the water I could see what appeared to be an island.

"That's The Great Orme," announced Thomas. It's really a headland with a hill on it. There's a cable car that goes up to the summit. I will take you there too."

As we sped along, I looked back along the way we had come to see the coastline swoop around behind me; in front another large craggy outcrop that looked as if we might crash into it and suddenly it went dark. I felt myself reach for Thomas' hand and I squeezed it tightly.

I allowed myself to let him keep hold of my hand as we emerged from the tunnel and back into the bright sunshine as the coast and our view of the sea unravelled before us.

"We are getting off at the next station."

The train whistled again as he spoke, and gradually slowed down, whisps of steam enveloping the mighty creature. "I think it's far enough for one day."

Penmaenmawr consisted of another very long expanse of beach and a village nestled in a valley with mountains behind. We walked up a narrow footpath called Constitution Hill, with cottages on one side and trees on the other, it was a very peaceful and pretty place and somewhat steep in places, finally emerging at a wider road at the top. We turned right at the top and walked along past a parade of little shops, to find the post office so that we could post our postcards.

"Happy now?" he laughed.

"I am," I replied. "I think we need a cup of tea and perhaps a piece of cake."

"We'll find a teashop," he suggested. "Do you know, some of the stone that we carry on the railway comes from here and slate from the quarries in Ffestiniog." Thomas was full of interesting information. "And this here is a memorial of Gladstone," he pointed out a bust of the four times Prime Minister that had been erected on a plinth with a wrought iron railing around. We walked along, turning right to go down Paradise Road. "He used to holiday here apparently."

"I can see the sea again from up here," I gasped at the sight. "How perfectly blue it is. Joe would love it here…and Lizzie, the sea air would do her the world of good."

Paradise Hill wound its way down the hillside towards the sea with the large hills behind us. We crossed over the rail track via the footbridge and walked along the promenade above the beach where we found a small tea house and ordered a fresh pot of tea and fresh cream cakes.

"I think we should head back to Rhyl when we have finished this, don't you?" he mumbled with his mouth full.

I looked up at him, tucking into his cake with gusto. "What is it with you and jam?" I laughed, handing him a napkin. "There is a huge dollop on your chin."

The train ride back to Rhyl was every bit as mesmerising as our outward journey and we arrived back at Mrs Lunns at half past five, just in time for tea.

The next couple of days were slow and lazy. We sauntered along the seafront and visited the Pavilion theatre where the Grand Jubilee organ, the world's largest organ was housed. The Victoria Pier was a very long structure, but we were not allowed to walk along its long length as it had been damaged, first by ships many years ago, but also by fire and then storms, it had been closed for ten years as it was unsafe. We visited the Marine Lake too, there was a funfair with rides and a zoo. The best feature of all was the miniature railway and Thomas was in his seventh heaven watching it. He was like a child when it stopped at the small station and we climbed on board to take our seats in the diminutive carriage behind the engine, the tiny beast chugging its way around the lake, the two of us laughing like children all the way around.

On the third morning, Thomas left me in the sitting room after breakfast, mysteriously saying he had something to do, and he would be back in an hour or so. I wandered into the pretty back garden to wait for him and took my place on a striped, blue deckchair, where I sat with my feet up reading a novel that I had found in a shop on the seafront. Mrs Lunn came out into the sunshine and handed me two postcards.

"I think this one was delayed yesterday but these are both for you." She spoke with a lilting Welsh accent, so warm and familiar to me and I wondered if Lizzie was enjoying herself with Aunt Emily and Cousin Harry.

"You look very relaxed and comfortable dearie," she said as she disappeared back inside to bake her bread for teatime.

I took them from her to read, the first one was from Ma, and the second from Emma and Joe.

Failsworth
Dear Daughter,
Just a card in answer to yours. Pleased to hear
you are enjoying yourselves and found all well as
it leaves me at present. Remember me to all.
Teddy as gone to Oswestry for a day to see
Lizzie.
Mother xxxx

I laughed as I looked at Emma's card, she had such a sense of humour, reading that it had been raining back home. I took up my book again to read until Thomas came back, but my mind wasn't on my story. He had been acting strange since breakfast and in a hurry to go out, constantly glancing at his pocket watch. He was a peculiar man at times.

Thomas returned an hour later as promised but refused to tell me where he had been, keeping suspiciously quiet.

"I say we stay in the garden and read our books in the sunshine," I suggested, frowning at his odd behaviour.

"A lazy day," he agreed, stretching out in the warmth and peace of the garden.

Often that afternoon he looked over to me, as if he wanted to speak, but then he stopped himself and continued to read his book.

"What is it, Thomas?" I asked, humoured by his performance. "Why are you acting strange? Do speak up, or you will bubble over!"

"No, not yet!" and he buried his head in his book again.

This continued for the rest of the day and over our teatime too. The fresh baked bread was delicious, thickly sliced ham, salad, and a hot pea soup. Mrs Lunn had made some buns that reminded me of the ones my Grandma Humphreys made all those years ago. Blissful memories at last flooded my relaxed and tranquil mind.

After tea we retired into the sitting room. The other guests were delayed in finishing their tea and we were alone.

"It is so very pleasant here," I said, seating myself on the small sofa, kicking off my soft shoes and placing my stockinged feet on a little stool in front of the empty grate. There was no need for a fire in the middle of summer, Mrs Lunn had arranged a beautiful basket of dried flowers and placed it on the hearth. The colours, as in my room matched the colours of the furnishings. Thomas stood behind the large, winged back gentleman's chair where he usually sat each evening.

"Aren't you sitting down?" I asked, starting to get a little uneasy with his behaviour. "My goodness Thomas, you've been strange all day, what's wrong?"

"Close your eyes," he said.

I closed my eyes, covering them with my hands as I used to do as a child when we played hide and seek.

In the quietness I heard him open a small cupboard in the corner of the room. I almost peeped through my fingers but decided against it as I felt a heavy weight being placed on my lap.

I deliberately stayed still, with my hands over my eyes; my turn to play.

"You can open them now," he said in a playful, eager voice.

On my knee was a large heavy box wrapped in brown paper, tied simply with a piece of twine. I looked up at his excited face; I had no idea what might be inside.

"What is it?"

"Open it," he urged, "open it and find out." He grinned at me; a huge stupid, wonderful, warm, and loving grin.

I pulled at the end of the twine to unravel the knot and carefully unfolded the brown paper. I lifted the lid. Inside the box was a large brown book. I reached inside to touch it and lovingly ran my fingers over the cover, which was embossed with two flowers and the words, *POSTCARD ALBUM* written in a fancy flowing script. The book was thick with empty paper pages, little slits cut in them where cards could be mounted.

I tenderly lifted the album from the box and held it, precious against my chest. It was heavy and solid.

I looked up at him again finding that I could not speak, I mouthed a simple "thank you."

"We could mount all your cards and mine together in here Beatrice," he said, falling on his knees beside me. He took my hand in his, holding it against his cheek.

"We can travel and collect many more postcards together, if you'll promise to be mine," he said, smiling at me.

I looked down deep into his soft sky-blue eyes, my smile was reflected in their depth, and I finally knew that I was safe.

* THE END *

Karol Darnell

All the postcards referred to are taken from
Beatrice's album and can
all be viewed on the publisher's website:
www.honestypress.co.uk

Lizzie passed away on 14th of November 1923 at the age of twenty-nine, two weeks before she was due to be married. It is not clear, nor remembered to whom she was to be married, but Teddy was the sender of many cards to both Lizzie and Beatrice in the album and so he has played that part in the story. Lizzie was laid to rest in the family grave with her sisters and stepfather Joe. **A D41**

> *Minnie Humphreys 5th October 1901*
> *Sarah Alice Ward 7th December 1903*
> *Sarah Annie Ward 10th June 1905*
> *Joe Ward 17th July 1907*
> *Eunice Humphreys 17th December 1914*
> *Elizabeth Alice Humphreys 17th November*
> *1923*

Beatrice and Thomas were married at St Johns Failsworth on the 5th of July 1924 with her brother Joe and Elizabeth Hankinson as witnesses. They continued to live at 5 South View until the new houses were built on Broadway, New Moston when they bought number 164 and named it 'Blaen Ty' meaning end house, a nod to her Humphreys' Welsh roots. They did travel and collected many more postcards together. These were mounted in the postcard album, now very tatty, but which held the key to the story of this little family. They enjoyed visiting friends on Rothsay, Isle of Skye and Pontefract in Yorkshire as well as Rhyl in North Wales as a foursome with Joe and Emma. Their marriage did not produce any children, a fact that Beatrice was very sad about. Thomas died on 16th of May 1970 with Beatrice joining him on 16th February 1988. Both were cremated and their ashes scattered in Hollinwood cemetery. Six months before Beatrice died, her will was re written, leaving her house to her home help and a small sum of money to her only niece, Eunice Alice (Ward).

After Beatrice married, Alice Ann moved, with Joe to live with Mr James Ashton, the husband of her long-time friend Margaret; Alice Ann had promised to look after him when Margaret died but decency decreed that they should marry, which they did in July 1925, and they lived together for 12 years until July 1937 when James died. Alice Ann passed away on the 1st of March 1956, having buried three husbands and five of her seven children. She lies in the churchyard at St Marys, New Moston.

Joe and Emma courted for fourteen years, finally tying the knot on the 29th of August 1936. They had wanted to marry earlier but Emma gave the money she had saved for her own wedding to her sister, Ada in September 1935 so that she could marry. Emma also traded the 'other mans' engagement ring for a set of cutlery for her own "bottom drawer'.

Emma and Joe were blessed with a daughter who was born one year later, on the 22nd of July 1937 and was named Eunice Alice after Joe's sister and beloved Ma. Her precious memories and stories behind the truths in this book were the inspiration and motivation behind it.

My grandfather Joe sadly passed away 16th of January 1957 aged only 54 with my grandmother Emma following him on 28th of September 1960 aged only 56 years old, before I ever had chance to know them. They are buried together with Emma's parents, Thomas William Butt and Ada (Shaw) in Failsworth Cemetery. **H H3**

Aunt Emily's, second husband Thomas Jones died on 10th of January 1934 and is buried in Western Rhyn churchyard, near Oswestry. Upon Emily's death on 12th March 1954, her son, Harry brought her home and she lies with her first husband Henry Roberts in Failsworth Cemetery. **A F27**. Cousin Harry passed away in 1996 and now lies in Western Rhyn church yard with his wife Dorothy. They too were childless.

Henry and Sarah Ward (Grandpa and Granny Ward) are together with their daughter Mary Ann and her husband Ernest Stott in Failsworth. **L L11**

James Humphreys, lies with his parents, George and Elizabeth and his sister, also called Elizabeth, in Failsworth **A C34**

Janie Melling died in February 1949 aged 56 from a burst appendix. Her sister Leah was with her in Ancoats Hospital when she died. Failsworth **G K24**

John James Hankinson is buried in grave **XXX1. A. 10** in the New Irish Farm Commonwealth War Cemetery, northeast of Ypres, Belgium. According to official records, 4500 soldiers were reburied at Irish New Farm Cemetery after the Armistice, as only 73 soldiers were originally buried there. John fell on the night of the 3rd of March 1918 and was previously buried in grave number 10 Paratonnerre Farm French Cemetery, Boesinghe, a Belgian military cemetery, 800 metres south of Lizerne village, which contained 13 soldiers from the UK who fell between December 1917 and March 1918. John was reinterred in September 1920 with two other soldiers who died alongside him and another Borders regiment soldier who had fallen two weeks after John.

Thomas later took Beatrice to Ypres, but she did not visit John's grave. She said she did not want to hurt Thomas. She never forgot her JJ, and had all his letters, medals and grave papers placed in her coffin, so that no one would know where he was. Her telling of his death was that *"he had swapped trenches with his friend because he was coming home soon, and only one bomb fell on the trench that night."*

Beatrice wasn't to know what historical research wizardry is now possible and I hope she would be happy with her story, and the knowledge that Pte John James Hankinson will always be remembered.

Epilogue

I stood next to Joe at the graveside. He was linking my arm as if for my support of him, I could feel him trembling. Thomas and Emma stood slightly to one side, not knowing what to say or how to comfort any of us. I looked up as they lowered Lizzie into her resting place, to see Teddy with his arm over Ma's shoulder.

We were all equally dry eyed in disbelief or perhaps acceptance of losing Lizzie at the age of twenty-nine. Her life had been short, but not as short as our other sisters already gone.

I tried to remember the daddy I barely knew. My Granny Ward who was always promising to teach me how to play the piano. Grandma Humphreys, Uncle Henry Roberts, Grandpa Ward, Mrs Ashton and so many more.

I thought back to that day long ago when I was only seven years old when we had lain a two-month-old baby, Sarah Alice, to rest with her sister; our darling happy little Minnie. Then only a year and a half later another sister Sarah Annie aged only five months old. Three innocent babies who hadn't stood a chance against poverty and the illnesses that befall the poor, the feeble and underprivileged. Three little sisters that I had loved with all my heart and lost before they ever knew life.

My Pa, Joe, who had loved Lizzie, Eunice, and me as his own and who grieved so much that the hurt had killed him. He died broken-hearted with loss when his family wasn't even grown up yet. He lies asleep forever.

I weep yet still more for my beautiful songbird of a sister, Eunice; barely sixteen and who had gone through so much pain and suffering. She died before she had a chance to love or grow old. She left a huge hole that will never be filled. Her sparkling laughter, her beautiful curls, and her angelic voice, all gone forever.

Then I think of my dear John, the husband I only shared eight days of married life with. That darling husband of mine, who naively followed his leaders into battle. Gallant, gullible, loyal, and patriotic to the last. Cannon fodder! He now lies alone in the cold earth of a foreign land surrounded by his trusting comrades and brothers in arms. All I have are his letters and postcards, his piano, and his gramophone.

And now my big sister, best friend, confidant, and partner in crime. My first love, Lizzie; my life companion, the happiest most playful frivolous girl who couldn't keep money in her pocket, but who never thought of herself, always buying ribbons or sweets for us or her friends. She will lie with them all under the spreading tearful drooping branches of the willow tree where we now stand again.

Ma, Joe and me, Emma, Thomas, and Teddy. Lost without them, but alive together with the future in front of us.

I reach out to take some soil and scattered it on the coffin top, not that far below us. The grave is full, as is my heart. Full of hurt and loss; full of pain, and defeat and aching; yet bursting with love and pride and memories.

I look over to Thomas, I am strengthened by his presence. A cold wind blew, lifting the fallen leaves from the grass, to toss and tumble them around as if they didn't matter. He pulled up the collar of his coat to shield himself against the November wind.

I couldn't feel the wind. I looked out from my eyes, but I didn't feel anything. There was another large gust and with it came the rain that had been promising all week.

"Tears from the sky," Ma always called them. She said that they were sent to water God's good earth so that the flowers could grow - whilst we live our days in the sun.

Acknowledgments:

Thank you firstly to my Great Aunt Beatrice, (Aunty Beatie), who's collection of postcards inspired this book and inadvertently told the story of her family's life. There were 341 cards in her battered album altogether so I could not use them all.

Thank you to my mother, Eunice, who's memories, recollections, and personal accounts of conversations she had with Beatrice, Alice Ann, Joe and Emma were the truths and motivation behind the stories. I also thank her for the words she once uttered when reprimanding me - 'you embroider the truth'. So, I did.

My dad Brian Darnell, whose love of family history and diligent research impassioned me. I feel his loss daily.

My husband, Dave, whose support, and patience were admirable. Our four wonderful sons, you have taught me the meaning of unconditional love.

My nephew Jayden who joined us in the research of local sites and eagerly awaited this book.

Thank you to all those who have supported me in my writing process, including my friends in the Monday Writers' group; with your help I continue to grow into a better writer. Dee Holland, and my good friends in her evening tutorial group, likewise.

Susan Knight, great niece of JJ Hankinson who visited his grave on the centenary of his great sacrifice.

Chris Connelly, graphic designer, a nice man I met on a train.

Karol has always been an avid reader and lover of words, writing poetry and short stories for her own amusement. Her interest in family history and the re-discovery of Beatrice's postcard album, inspired this book as her first published novel. She is currently researching her next book; details to follow on the publisher's website:

www.honestypress.co.uk

She currently lives in Worcestershire and is married with four grown up sons.

Printed in Poland
by Amazon Fulfillment
Poland Sp. z o.o., Wrocław